THE COMPLETE GUIDE TO GERMAN SHEPHERDS

David Daigneault

www.lpmedia.org

Publication Data

David Daigneault

The Complete Guide to German Shepherds---- First edition.

Summary: "Successfully raising a German Shepherd dog from puppy to old age" --- Provided by publisher.

ISBN: 978-1-09042-033-6

[1. German Shepherds --- Non-Fiction] I. Title.

This book has been written with the published intent to provide accurate and author-itative information in regard to the subject matter included. While every reasonable pre-caution has been taken in preparation of this book the author and publisher expressly dis-claim responsibility for any errors, omissions, or adverse effects arising from the use or application of the information contained inside. The techniques and suggestions are to be used at the reader's discretion and are not to be considered a substitute for professional veterinary care. If you suspect a medical problem with your dog, consult your veterinarian.

Design by Sorin Rădulescu

First paperback edition, 2019

Cover Photo Courtesy of Joe Hanson

For Cody,
thanks for the life lessons -

TABLE OF CONTENTS

INTRODUCTION:

Full disclosure time. I am not a dog trainer or breeder. My professional qualifications are simply as a long-time lover of dogs and a five-year intensive course of study. Five years of guiding my German Shepherd, Cody, from a tentative eight-week-old toddler to his present ambitious adult stage of five years old and counting.

Owning a dog is a life-long commitment, and as part of that obligation I feel it is important to share what I know with as many people as possible. Some of my canine knowledge comes from the School of Hard Knocks. My wife and I made mistakes along the way. German Shepherds can be stubborn; they certainly have minds of their own and they don't hesitate to make a decision if you can't. So there a couple of things to bear in mind as you go though this book. Your German Shepherd will only know what you have taught him, good or bad. If you have left it up to him to amuse himself and he digs holes in the yard, that's not his fault, it's yours. Some of my knowledge comes from trainers, other dog owners, and yes, even books. When you commit to bringing a German Shepherd puppy home, get ready for the ride of your life. They will love you and they will never leave you. What more can you ask?

Remember, one of the best traits a dog has is his worldview. To your four-footed companion every day is a new day. There is a freshness and an eagerness to going out the front door to explore the world. It can look like the same path every day to you but to your dog it's a whole world of smells, sights, and sounds to sample that weren't there yesterday. A rabbit runs across the path and your dog will chase it like he has never seen one before.

All this is a way of saying that dogs bring a completely different perspective to approaching life. They invite you to live in the moment. They enjoy what is happening right now and aren't worried about the mortgage or the project at work that you are falling behind on. They're so lucky that they don't have to learn to be that way, it just comes naturally to them. So next time you're out and about, walking with your dog, try examining everything that surrounds you through their eyes. It will do you a world of good.

The good Shepherd dog knows his master almost better than himself and must wonder indeed at the lack of the reverse.

Max von Stephanitz

CHAPTER 1
German Shepherd Saga

Photo Courtesy of Nanc Schutte

As their name tells us, German Shepherds were originally bred to be working, herding dogs. The man who gets credit for establishing the GSD (German Shepherd Dog) as a distinct breed is an innovative thinker named Max von Stephanitz. The canine-obsessed, former German army cavalry captain was attending a dog show in the late 1800s when he saw a yellow and black tail-wagger that he fell in love with. Von Stephanitz was a big believer that dogs should have jobs. He also believed in rules and order. He could see the potential in Hektor, as that pioneering dog was named at the time, and bought him on the spot. Von Stephanitz had been working on a cooperative breeding program for many years that sought to create uniform working dog lines in Germany. He had met with limited success. In other words, he was trying to standardize an occupation, a hobby for some, that was a bit of a free-for-all. If you'll pardon the heresy of using a feline expression in a dog book, what von Stephanitz was attempting was sort of like herding cats. When he laid eyes on Hektor he knew he had found his ultimate prototype. Hektor measured about twenty-five inches at the withers (top of the shoulder) and certainly resembles today's German Shepherd, but looking at pictures of him you might almost imagine some wolf in his background as well. That may be for good reason because there is a long-standing rumor that Hektor had wolf blood in his family tree.

Hektor would go on to have his name changed to something more romantically appropriate for a stud. He became Horand von Grafrath and formed the centerpiece of a breeding program that emphasized physical strength, intelligence, and loyalty. Von Stephanitz went on to create the German Shepherd Association (Verein für Deutsche Schäferhunde), which established breed standard guidelines. Horand von Grafrath had the honor of becoming the first registered "Deutsche Schaferhunde," or German Shepherd dog. Oh yes, and one more thing. Von Stephanitz valued tenacity. That attribute combined with the rest of the genetic package made German Shepherds the ideal canine for the next stage of their development. They were to become the dogs of war.

War Dogs

World War One. The war to end all wars, as it was ironically known. GSDs were part of the German military when hostilities commenced in 1914. The use of the canines was new and had been suggested by, you guessed it, Captain Max von Stephanitz. The dogs played a variety of roles during the bloody conflict, including acting as messengers, ammunition carriers, and sentries. The Red Cross also used German Shepherds as casualty dogs, finding wounded soldiers in the mayhem of battle. The attributes of strength, intelligence, and fearlessness, so long admired by von Stephanitz, made German Shepherds the ideal military animal to serve in a deadly atmosphere of tremendous noise, danger, and constant turmoil. Some estimates indicate that by the end of the Great War upwards of fifty thousand dogs had been used by both the Germans and Allied powers.

FUN FACT
Star-Spangled Shepherd

German Shepherds were first used by U.S. Armed Forces in WWII. They served as guards and search and rescue dogs, as well as messengers between soldiers. Prior to this, in WWI, German Shepherds served in the German military. It was the notable performance of these dogs for the German Army which impressed the American and English armed forces and led them to develop their own military training programs for German Shepherds. Today, this breed continues to be a valuable part of the military and has served with military police as well as Navy SEAL Teams.

At the end of hostilities in 1918 all three major players at the time, the Germans, British, and Americans, were working on individual programs designed to develop specific roles for, and integrate GSDs into, the working military. This is also the time when, because of the German Shepherd's wide exposure during the war, the breed's popularity took off. Nothing reflects the American public's affinity for the GSD more than the cinematic phenomena of Rin Tin Tin and Strongheart.

Strongheart was a casualty of war in much the same way as many humans after 1918. The large, male GSD had served in the German Red Cross during the conflict but his owner, who was destitute when hostilities ceased, couldn't afford to keep him. Luckily, Strongheart's owner had a friend in New York who had a kennel, so Strongheart was shipped to him. Like many human movie stars Strongheart was "discovered" by a film director and ultimately made six popular adventure films in the early twenties. Strongheart died in 1929, but not before propelling the GSD into the dreams and imaginations of countless filmgoers.

Strongheart

Strongheart may have been the first cinematic dog star but he was soon to be eclipsed by an even larger canine talent. Arguably, Rin Tin Tin's biggest break came when as a puppy he was rescued by a U.S. soldier in France during World War One and later brought back to California. Rin Tin Tin and his owner, Lee Duncan, soon found their way into silent movies. By the late 1920s, Rinty, as Duncan affectionately called his furry companion, was making more than five thousand dollars a week and had a private chef. The four-footed movie actor died in 1932 but by then had more than twenty-five films under his collar and had top billing in his own radio show, appropriately titled The Wonder Dog.

When World War Two broke out, dogs, and especially GSDs, were in the thick of the action. While they were utilized by both sides in the conflict it is perhaps the grim image of the Nazi regime with its secret police, the Gestapo, rounding up people using ferocious, barking German Shepherds that is embedded in many imaginations. This may also be the point in time where the "Big Bad German Shepherd" stereotype surfaced, which is still with us today. More about that in Chapter Three, German Shepherd Stigma.

One of the more amazing tales about heroic hounds from the Second World War revolves around the 13th Parachute Battalion of the British Army. They had a dog named Bing, who was a German Shepherd mix. Bing was a graduate of the British War Dog Training School and

Rin Tin Tin

had been taught to jump out of planes wearing his parachute. This "para-dog" jumped into battle in France on D-Day. His areas of expertise were locating minefields and being able to sniff out hidden enemy soldiers. Bing survived the war and was given Britain's highest honor for animals that have displayed "conspicuous bravery."

There are many stirring war dog stories from the Second World War but at least one more deserves mentioning. Another German Shepherd mix named Chips served with U.S. forces during the invasion of Sicily in 1943. The fearless hound attacked a machine gun

German Shepherd in WWII

nest, chomping on the German soldiers there and upending the machine gun from its mount. All the Germans at the scene surrendered to the U.S. Army and Chips escaped with minor injuries. The daring dog was later recommended for several military honors including the Silver Star and a Purple Heart. And one last Chips note: when General Dwight Eisenhower, then Supreme Allied Commander in Europe, bent down to give him a congratulatory pat, the war dog Chips bit the military man as he had apparently been trained to do to strangers who approached him. At least in this case, Chips got away with biting the hand that fed him.

After two world wars the population of German Shepherds and their owners in Germany had been decimated. It took breeders there years of effort to bring back a population of dogs that displayed the traits that von Stephanitz had so tirelessly worked toward. In the meantime the popularity of the breed continued to skyrocket in North America. The Adventures of Rin Tin Tin dominated the television airwaves from 1954 to 1959. The GSD was in the top ten popular dogs in the 1950s. With all this fame and glory, though, came a different set of problems. While European breeders had followed von Stephanitz's established guidelines, American breeders had not. This meant that while North American breeders focused on the appearance of the dog, sporting a larger frame, with sloped backs for show, European breeders concentrated on physical strength, intelligence, and loyalty. This divergence brings us to the two worlds of the German Shepherd of today.

Photo Courtesy of Ashni Rana

The GSD Now

While many of us may look at a dog and say "oh, that's a German Shepherd," in the GSD world it is a little more complicated than that. In fact, there are considered to be five distinct lines of German Shepherds, each with their own look and temperament. When you are looking for a puppy you might want to delve into the specific background of the breeder you are dealing with. Based on the various lines and the breeder's specific involvement she should be able to tell you what the physical characteristics of your puppy will be as an adult and also what the "mindset" of the dog will be. They could be characterized as a "family dog" with "medium drive," for instance. I'll use my own German Shepherd, Cody, as an example. He comes from a breeder who specializes in longer-coated dogs, with large square heads and calmer demeanors. The breeder characterizes Cody as having the look of an old-style "Schaferhund" with a straight back and she boasts imported dogs in her breeding program. Let's contrast Cody's appearance to the first of the five GSD lines on our list.

a) American show lines

This line of dogs comes in for a fair amount of criticism. They have been bred mainly for show and the animals have a much narrower head than their European counterparts. Perhaps the single most distinguishing feature would be the severely sloping back end, something dog experts call "angulation." In theory, with well-bred animals, the temperament will be calmer than a working line of dog, with somewhat less energy, which may make them more suitable as a family dog. The criticism concerning this line of GSD is that they have been overbred for show characteristics, resulting in health concerns that can prematurely shorten a dog's life. Two of the major problems are hip and elbow dysplasia. Dysplasia occurs when the joints do not form properly, allowing them to partially dislocate. This is mainly a genetic condition. Indiscriminate and "backyard" breeding geared to profit and not for the animal's benefit has also harmed the image of the GSD in North America. The American show line dog will be heavier and taller than the European dogs.

b) Czech working lines

These dogs originate from what was then known as Czechoslovakia (now the Czech Republic and Slovakia). This branch of GSD has darker, uniform coloring with black, brown, and gray predominating. Their ears will seem small compared to the radar-like appendages seen on some North American dogs. Czech working line GSDs have great agility and a powerful build. They were originally used for border patrol and security. They have straight backs and exhibit high energy levels.

c) East German DDR working lines

The Czech dogs and East German shepherds have closely related genetics but there are some differences. The DDR line of dogs is mostly dark in color, with some red. They possess big heads, a large chest, and high stamina levels. After World War Two when Germany was partitioned, the Communist state assumed control of the breeding and registration of German Shepherds in their jurisdiction. They were rigorously bred as working dogs capable of long security shifts, including tracking and attacking people attempting to flee East Germany.

d) West German working lines

This line of the GSD family originates in what was post-war West Germany. Somewhat like their DDR counterparts, they were bred for guarding and working with the armed forces and law enforcement. The color will vary but they can be saddlebacks with black and tan perhaps with some red. Their hindquarters will not be flat and will have some angulation but not to the extent of their North American cousins. Their drive may not be quite as high as the eastern Shepherds'.

e) West German show lines

These dogs aren't as dark in their coloration as their eastern cousins and generally will have a saddleback design usually with black and red predominating. Their back will have some slope. They are generally healthier than the American dogs because of the German Shepherd Dog Association guidelines that place an emphasis on hip and elbow certification in breeding dogs. They have a somewhat stockier build and their faces will not be as narrow as North American Shepherds.

- On average, GSD males range from twenty-four to twenty-six inches at the shoulder and weigh from sixty-five to ninety pounds.

- On average, GSD females range from twenty-two to twenty-four inches at the shoulder and weigh from fifty to seventy pounds.

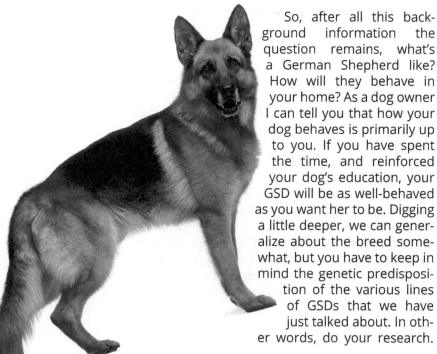

So, after all this background information the question remains, what's a German Shepherd like? How will they behave in your home? As a dog owner I can tell you that how your dog behaves is primarily up to you. If you have spent the time, and reinforced your dog's education, your GSD will be as well-behaved as you want her to be. Digging a little deeper, we can generalize about the breed somewhat, but you have to keep in mind the genetic predisposition of the various lines of GSDs that we have just talked about. In other words, do your research.

You can never read too much about the breed of dog you are thinking about and you can never ask too many questions. In the German Shepherd's case the breeding line is also important. If a breeder is reluctant to answer questions it may be time to look for another breeder.

German Shepherds are not like any other dog you might acquire. They are smart, they want to learn, they have boundless energy, and they want lots of your time. If you can't deal with that package don't get a German Shepherd. I see ads every day by people attempting to "re-home" their GSD because they can't devote the time, or their circumstances have changed and they can no longer keep the dog. To me that's like saying they can no longer afford to feed a family member and they have to go. Think long and hard about your decision to get a large, demanding dog like a German Shepherd. If you decide to get one for all the right reasons, you will have a partner and best friend for life. I'll give you some things to think about in the next chapter that will help you make your dog decision.

CHAPTER 2
Is the German Shepherd right for you?

"Far too often I see people go out and get a German Shepherd because their neighbor or friend had one that they really liked, or because they love their look, or because they've fallen for the tales of their courage. But you really need to do your research with this breed. You need to understand their needs and whether they will truly fit your lifestyle. Get ready for a smart dog that will walk all over you if they know you won't be consistent with them. They need to be worked and they need a job, they are a working breed and as such they can go stir crazy and become destructive if not exercised appropriately."

Celeste Schmidt
Dakonic German Shepherds

There are few things more enjoyable than a thoroughly socialized, well-trained German Shepherd. This breed is handsome, intelligent, loyal, protective, athletic, humorous, and creative. They are excellent companions and GSDs never tire of your company. Those are just some of the things they give to you. In return they require some basic things in order to become good canine citizens. That's where you have to pay back. Let's go through what you need to think about before taking that fateful step of bringing a German Shepherd into your home. Yes, puppies are cute and everybody loves the little guys, but they don't stay that way for very long. You'll soon have an eighty-pound dog on your hands who looks to you for guidance.

How much time do you have to devote to your dog? These are some

Photo Courtesy of Carrie Anderson

of the things you need to think about seriously in advance of D-day, or dog day. Let's see if you can handle the pressure.

Exercise

A German Shepherd isn't content to hang around the house all day. They need stimulation and exercise. Every day. At our house, my dog, Cody, goes out a minimum of five times a day. Two of those walks will be for thirty minutes or more. Some of those walks will involve ball games such as playing "soccer," definitely his favorite sport. The dog goes outside, rain, snow, no matter the weather. GSDs can handle most conditions so that means you need to be prepared to go out multiple times, on a regular basis, in all types of weather. That's just part of the exercise package. A dog who gets lots of exercise and is tired at the end of the day is a good dog. However, physical exercise isn't the only type of exertion your dog needs. Mental exercise is also necessary for your pet. Reinforcing commands, ball games, and learning new tricks all contribute to tiring him out. If you and you family can't commit to an adequate minimum amount of physical and mental exercise, then don't consider a German Shepherd.

Maintenance

Your pup may be a wonder dog but there are some things she can't do for herself. Your dog should be brushed out once a day. That helps to remove excess hair, and if your GSD has a longer coat it prevents matting. From my experience this breed doesn't require a lot of bath time. In fact, less is more as you don't want to remove the essential oils that help keep a dog's skin healthy. Two or three times a year is more than adequate unless they have encountered some unfriendly wildlife, like skunks. You need to be prepared to administer heartworm, flea, and tick medication as needed. Regular teeth brushing is a must. Dogs are susceptible to tartar buildup and if you let it get out of control it will necessitate a trip to the vet. Speaking of veterinarians, an annual checkup at a minimum is mandatory for your GSD. You will almost certainly have more frequent trips when your dog is a puppy. So pet insurance makes a lot of sense.

Education and Training

You should probably put a puppy training class on your agenda. That will not only help socialize your youngster but it will give you some good habits to build into your daily schedule. You will need to be the leader as far as your dog is concerned. German Shepherds are always watching you, looking for cues. They want to know what is expected of them and they look for you to give direction. Remember, they are perfectly capable of making decisions for themselves if you don't step up. You may not want to live with the consequences of your GSD calling the shots. Further training, either in a group class or individually, is a good idea if you can afford it. Whatever you learn in class should be passed along to family members for reinforcement.

Quality Time

Your dog should be considered part of the family and as such needs to spend as much quality time with his pack as possible. He should go most places that you go. Don't forget there are many pet friendly stores that welcome dogs. Your GSD should also be welcome to lie on the rug and watch TV with the family. I've caught Cody more than once intently watching the action on the screen. GSDs are people dogs and want to be with you. Also make sure family members are all on the same page with getting your new family member. Dogs don't make good gifts so no

GSDs under the tree for Christmas. It also helps give everyone ownership if every household member has a dog-related chore. Call it quality time with Rex.

Photo Courtesy of Andrea Liu

Living Space

You need to have a suitable home for your dog. While I have heard stories of GSDs living in apartments, I would suggest that is not the most suitable living arrangement for them. They need inside room as well as outside space. A house with a large, fenced in yard is desirable; a country property would be considered paradise. If you're renting, remember landlords aren't big fans of GSDs. Don't get a GSD if your living situation isn't stable and a move might be in your future. German Shepherds like routine; they like knowing what to expect. Can you blame them?

Expenses

German Shepherds are big dogs. They are also a big expense. You need to be prepared to pay the freight for your best friend. Establishing a budget is a must. The ongoing costs for your adult dog can easily exceed two thousand dollars a year and be even more depending on the animal's health and the type of diet your GSD is on. This doesn't take into account start-up expenses incurred in the initial period of pet ownership such as toys, a crate, leashes, collars, and food and water bowls. I'll break the costs down for you later in Chapter 5.

Motivation

This last area is the most important. Don't get a German Shepherd because you think they would make a good macho accessory. Do get one if you are looking for a dog that you will love as a family member. That's for the life of the animal. GSDs can live twelve to fourteen years of age so bringing one home is not a short-term commitment.

Buying or Adopting

"I personally feel that both reputable breeders and reputable rescues offer dogs to meet everyone's needs. As a reputable breeder of the German Shepherd, I would recommend people consider temperament, energy levels, and drive that best suits their needs over the dog's color and bloodlines."

Erika Martin
Century Farms

It's a sad fact. There are hundreds of thousands of dogs in shelters and rescues around North America. Many of them are at risk of euthanasia because no one seems to want them. Here are some less than heartwarming statistics from the American Society for the Prevention of Cruelty to Animals (ASPCA).

- About 3.3 million dogs enter the shelter system each year
- 670,000 of those animals are euthanized

Photo Courtesy of
Nicole Grethen

Many dogs that end up in shelters are purebreds and if you look at any listings from shelters or rescues you will see quite a few German Shepherd faces. They're there because of the following reasons, once again as outlined by the ASPCA.

- Problematic behaviors
- Aggressive behaviors
- Grew larger than expected
- Health problems owner couldn't handle

Shelter dogs aren't bad dogs; they just haven't had very responsible owners. Unfortunately, the dogs pay the price. So, if you're looking for a companion and don't have specific requirements in mind, then an adopted dog may be just the ticket for you. Typically, adoption fees are relatively inexpensive, perhaps several hundred dollars for a purebred. However, when you compare that to breeders' prices of a thousand dollars or more, rescue animals are more than affordable. Considering an adult GSD from a shelter gives you a chance to see the size of the animal, gauge her personality, perhaps even spend some time with the animal so you can get a feel for her temperament. Those are all good things associated with adopting.

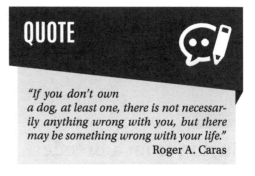

QUOTE

"If you don't own a dog, at least one, there is not necessarily anything wrong with you, but there may be something wrong with your life."
Roger A. Caras

There is one major con you need to know about. You can never know the extent to which the animal's previous life has affected it. Everything from separation anxiety to fear of males (perhaps because of abuse). Be prepared that your rescue German Shepherd may require some extra patience. So, if you do adopt you are taking on some unknowns but if you are thinking about a German Shepherd in the first place, you should be a strong enough individual to handle some turbulence. If you want a GSD, and there are too many in the shelter system, and you could save a life, it just might be the best decision you ever made. For everyone concerned.

Photo Courtesy of Mika Lee

Buying from a Breeder

There is no shortage of breeders out there. Unfortunately, however, there is a shortage of reputable breeders so it's important to do your homework. Some things to consider:

- Make sure you're signing a contract that spells out obligations for both parties.
- The breeder should offer a health guarantee (regarding hip and elbow dysplasia).
- The breeder should be prepared to offer references to people who have purchased pups from her.
- Are the parents available to be seen? The mother (or dam) should be on premises at the very least.
- Both parents should have official registrations.
- There should be a waiting list for puppies.
- There should be no more than one or two litters produced a year.

In my search for a pup, for instance, I went to dog shows to talk to breeders and look at various dogs. You might also want to check in with your local veterinarian to see if they have any breeder recommendations to make based on their personal experience. There are many German Shepherd clubs out there. Even if there isn't one in your area, making contact and talking to a member about your situation can be an invaluable source of information to you. Word of mouth can also be a good a source of GSD intelligence. I run into people almost every week who have German Shepherds and who are only too happy to show you pictures and talk about which breeder they purchased from. Taking a stroll to your local dog park puts you into a canine environment that can be eye-opening as well as bringing you into contact with all kinds of dog people.

One of the very first things I did in my dog hunt, after doing countless hours of research, was go and visit the breeder that I had zeroed in on. Make sure you pay attention to the breeder's home environment. Check out the condition of the other dogs present, and ask every question you can think of. There are no stupid questions. Examine any puppies to see how well maintained they are. Notice how lively they seem to be and how eager they are to check you out. The breeder should have lots of questions for you as well. They should be looking out for their pups' welfare and wanting to make sure they go to suitable homes. The breeder should also offer to take your dog back if your circumstances change and you can't keep them any longer.

The Decision

"Ask the breeder questions about the dog's temperament, what training the parents have had and what titles their dogs have earned. It will give you a good idea of what the puppy's temperaments with be. Ask the breeder for an explanation of each of the puppies in the litters temperament and which puppy is best suited for your lifestyle. Some puppies are more active, while others are calmer."

Katie Halfen
Casamoko Shepherds

If you have your heart set on a German Shepherd and you've decided to go ahead, it will help for you to think about the dog you want instead of just a dog. Here's what I mean by that. Once again, I'll use my own experience. When my wife and I talked about getting a puppy we knew we wanted a family dog, one with a sociable disposition that we wouldn't have to shut away somewhere to keep visitors safe. So, when we talked to our breeder, we very quickly identified that she bred her dogs for a "calm, sound temperament" and to be a "family companion." That's what we wanted.

So, identify the qualities your family is looking for. Remember the five lines of GSDs that I talked about in Chapter One. You can find breeders here and abroad that can supply German Shepherds with different attributes and drives. If you are looking to compete then you may want a Shepherd with a higher drive. It's all a matter of why you want the dog and then matching with the right breeder. It might take some time to find the right kennel but take your time and get it right. Remember, it's for life.

To Breed or Not

One of the most important decisions you will make regarding your GSD is whether you intend to breed your dog. That's a choice that shouldn't be undertaken lightly. Remember all the dogs in shelters and the high rate of euthanasia? The contract with your breeder should include a spay/neuter clause and if you decide not to spay/neuter, the purchase price of your German Shepherd will be higher. When contemplating whether to have a litter you need to take into account all the responsible attributes you expected your breeder to have when you bought your puppy. You will need to look for a suitable purebred mate for your GSD. I mean you bought a purebred for a reason, right? And by suitable, I mean one that has been cleared health-wise; certified clear of DM (degenerative myelopathy) and dysplasia, for example. The mate should also have a social temperament that lends itself to well-adjusted puppies. After those considerations you'll need to assemble a checklist and strictly adhere to it. A checklist should include the following.

Breeding Checklist

- ✔ Do you have the time to devote to your breeding project? You know it will always take more time than you thought.
- ✔ Make sure you are prepared for the financial implications of bringing puppies into the world. Average GSD litter size is eight.
- ✔ Those puppies will require all kinds of maintenance and socialization time.
- ✔ Just as you were scrutinized before buying your dog you need to screen your potential buyers.
- ✔ The puppies will find their way into your heart but they have to go to their forever homes. Prepare for the emotional toll that will take.
- ✔ All responsible breeders will take dogs back that the owners can no longer care for. Are you prepared to do that?
- ✔ No female dogs (bitches) under two years old to be bred. No male dogs (studs) under eighteen months.

This is not by any means a comprehensive list but hopefully gives you an idea of what it takes to responsibly breed even one litter of puppies. In the next chapter we'll go into why some people consider German Shepherds to be the bad boys on the block. I'll also give you some thoughts about what you, as a new GSD owner, can do about what I call the Shepherd Stigma.

CHAPTER 3
German Shepherd Stigma

Photo Courtesy of Jenny Bowden

L et me start this chapter with a story. Several years ago, my then eight-month-old German Shepherd, Cody, and I were enrolled in an obedience class for young dogs. Once a week we would pile into the truck and drive to the nearest small city where the classes were held. Cody, thank goodness, was over his car sickness stage at this point. Anyway, there was a dynamic present in the class that took me a couple of weeks to fully appreciate.

First, just a little bit of backstory. My wife, Cody, and I live on a country property of about five and a half acres with no dogs in the neighborhood for Cody to socialize with. So, we always made a point of taking him places to see people and other dogs. One thing Cody has never gotten over is when he enters a new place or somewhere he hasn't been for a while, he always lets out a loud bark or two. Could be the veterinarian office, could be the pet food store, it doesn't matter. Big bark and then settle down. More or less.

So back to the obedience class. After the first session or two, and the barks that went with them, it was suggested that I bring Cody in right at the beginning of class, but not earlier, so as not to disturb the other dogs as much. Cody's classmates were a mixture of chihuahuas, golden retrievers, and poodles. He was the biggest and loudest. He always calmed down as the instruction went on because he had work to do.

After the second class I noticed that all the other dogs and their owners were lining up on the other side of the room as far away from Cody as they could get. The lessons went on like this for the requisite eight weeks. When I inquired about the next, advanced class, I was told politely that the other owners were afraid of my dog and so they would rather I not come to any more classes. I was later informed by a friend of mine who helped run some of the classes that because Cody was a "big, loud, aggressive German Shepherd," he wasn't welcome. So that was my first taste of what I call the "German Shepherd Stigma." Where does this stereotype come from and why is it still with us today? Here's what I think.

FUN FACT
Ready to Serve

Because of their strength, intelligence, and loyal disposition, German Shepherds are one of the most popular breeds to be employed as service dogs. In the United States, it's estimated that approximately half a million service dogs are helping people with disabilities. By helping people with physical handicaps, emotional support needs, and psychiatric disorders, service dogs are saving lives every day.

Some people are just afraid of dogs, especially big dogs. No doubt about it. Merriam-Webster's dictionary defines cynophobia as a "morbid fear of dogs." Some psychologists have theorized that as much as 10 percent of the population suffers from this phobia. But I think the "German Shepherd Stigma" runs deeper than that. For instance, for much of the older demographic, GSDs are "police dogs," with the intimidating reputation that accompanies that image.

Of course, every dog has his day. Big dogs, I mean. Dobermans have been dumped on as snarling, aggressive bullies. Rottweilers have been ranted about as vicious thugs. More recently, Pit Bulls have been pummeled as biting bullies. GSDs are different though. All through this wave of big, bad dogs that society seems to continually wash over us is interwoven the constant image of the snarling, snapping German Shepherd.

Think back to all those World War Two movies you might have watched. Concentration camps, prisoner of war camps with armed soldiers patrolling the perimeters. With dogs. What kind of dogs? Well big, bad German Shepherds, of course. Fast forward to Cold War–era Eastern Europe and who is patrolling the borders keeping communism safe from democracy? German Shepherds again. GSDs have an imposing reputation as guard and security dogs and as excellent K-9 partners with the military and law enforcement. That image works against the breed in many ways. You can't be a tough guy and a loving family pet at the same time, right? Wrong!

It so happens GSDs can be tough guys and big softies at the same time. I know that. I suspect you know that if you want to bring a German Shepherd into your home to live with you and your family. So, although we know there are no bad dogs, only irresponsible owners, and that you can't paint an entire breed with the same brush, it happens. Urban legend, "Black Dog Syndrome," call it what you will, has manifested itself

Photo Courtesy of
Jamie Nicholson

in many states and municipalities enacting Breed Specific Legislation, or BSL. This kind of law usually has two parts. BSL can either consist of an outright ban on certain breeds or restrictions placed on a certain type of dog. Those limitations can include:

- The dog has to wear a certain type of collar or other identifying marker that indicates she is a "vicious and aggressive" dog

- Owners are required to purchase a specific amount of liability insurance

- The dog must be spayed or neutered

- Muzzles are mandatory

- Warning signs need to be displayed where dog lives

- Only certain secure leashes may be used on the "dangerous" breed

- Special licensing requiring more expensive fees

- Banned from using certain public spaces

- Microchip or tattoo mandatory

- Obligation to file photos of dog and owner with municipal authorities

In addition, many insurance companies refuse to give homeowners insurance if they have any one of a number of "high risk" breeds that appear on the prohibited list. German Shepherds appear on almost every company's list. As well, landlords may refuse prospective tenants because they have a black and tan baby.

So, by now I think you get the picture. You have just discovered that being a GSD owner is a challenge on a whole different level. You thought you just had to deal with a willful, headstrong dog that if not properly trained is big enough to drag you around the block without even breaking a sweat. However, there are some things you can do about the "German Shepherd Stigma." Things that will combat the stereotype and make life better for owners, and the dogs themselves. Catch your breath, and then read on.

Stemming the Stigma

Let me pose a loaded question. If I were to ask you to name the three most aggressive dog breeds, what would you say? Now we know some dogs have been bred to be more aggressive. Yes, German Shepherds can be high drive, it's in their DNA, but let's get back to the question. These are the top three most aggressive breeds, according to a study done by researchers at the University of Pennsylvania:

1. Dachshund

2. Chihuahua

3. Jack Russell

What's my point? Well, as dog owners we need to be continually educating ourselves, so that if you find yourself in a discussion with someone who isn't as enamoured of your GSD as you are, you can help them understand the difference between myth and reality. Every breed has unique characteristics that are more or less common, but all dogs are individuals and have their own personalities. You can help people understand that. That's part one to helping combat the societal stigma out there about German Shepherds and other powerful breed dogs. Here's part two. You need to be the most responsible dog owner out there. If you are, your dog will be the most obedient, well-socialized, well-respected hound on the block.

- Train your dog early and often. The natural inclination of a GSD is to look to you for guidance. During your training you can reinforce the dog's nature to always be watching you and taking your cues. If they are looking at you, preferably watching your eyes, that means they aren't distracted and are likely to follow your direction. German Shepherds want to please and there is no

Photo Courtesy of Mya Milbury

*Photo Courtesy of
Anita Conklin*

one they want praise from more than you.

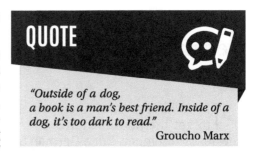

QUOTE

"Outside of a dog, a book is a man's best friend. Inside of a dog, it's too dark to read."
Groucho Marx

- Be effusive in your praise but when your GSD steps out of line make sure to correct him every time. Don't give anyone an excuse to point at your dog and say, "See, I told you so." Especially make sure you shut down mouthiness and nipping early on.

- Remember discipline and boundaries come first, then love and affection.

- When you are out with your German Shepherd don't be afraid to demonstrate how well-behaved they are, especially at dog parks. If people see your dog under control that goes a long way to dispelling the German Shepherd Stigma.

- If people approach you and want to pet your GSD and talk about the breed, make sure you're comfortable with that. Shepherds can be aloof and not much interested in humans other than their own pack so make sure you know your dog before allowing strangers hands on.

- While dogs can be dependable you can never trust them 100%. When it comes to children, especially other people's kids, never leave them unsupervised with your GSD. Never assume that your dog will behave in a certain way. Just because they have done something one hundred times before there is always that small chance.

- If you have the opportunity or the desire to make your German Shepherd an ambassador for her breed, think of training your dog for some kind of service. GSDs make excellent working dogs. Imagine the positive public relations it is every time a German Shepherd walks into a retirement residence as a therapy dog. Big dog, but lots of big smiles too.

As a German Shepherd owner, you will always have to work just a little bit harder than the other guy. If we all just do a little bit to counter that "big, bad German Shepherd" stereotype maybe one day the stigma will be relegated to the past. In fact, right now let's leave all the stigma discussion behind and look ahead. You've made your decision. You're getting a GSP (German Shepherd puppy). You sort of know what you're in for. Now let's talk about what you need to do to get ready to welcome your inquisitive toddler into your home. Safely.

CHAPTER 4
Getting Ready

If you have children then you already know some of what it takes to get the house, and your household, ready for the arrival of a new family member. But a German Shepherd puppy is a little bit different. Even at eight weeks, which is the earliest you should bring your GSP home, the nose rules.

✔ A dog's nose has as many as 300 million scent receptors.

✔ A human's nose has a mere 5 million.

That's why they are so preoccupied with following a trail. That's also how they get into trouble, especially as a pup. Let's look at some ways you can begin to keep your German Shepherd puppy safe even before you bring him home.

Photo Courtesy of
Celeste Schmidt
Dakonic GSDs

Preparing Puppy's Place

One of the things you're going to want to do is choose a room in the house that will be the primary living area for your GSP for the first while. You'll need to select a room with flooring material that is easily cleaned. There will be lots of "accidents" to deal with so be prepared. In our house, Cody's initial space was the entrance porch, which has old-school linoleum floors. One of the best choices we ever made. We also installed a baby gate which enabled us to keep the puppy confined to that room. Don't forget those little claws will scratch almost any flooring material so don't select a room with your prized hardwood floor; if the wood wasn't distressed before, it certainly will be after the little guy has been around for a while.

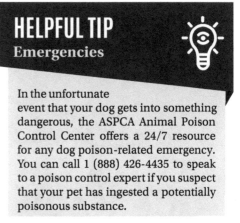

HELPFUL TIP

Emergencies

In the unfortunate event that your dog gets into something dangerous, the ASPCA Animal Poison Control Center offers a 24/7 resource for any dog poison-related emergency. You can call 1 (888) 426-4435 to speak to a poison control expert if you suspect that your pet has ingested a potentially poisonous substance.

You'll also want to make sure you have some comfortable chairs in that room because you will spend a lot of time there. There should be a door off that room that allows immediate access to the outside. This will make it easier when you start potty training in earnest. German Shepherds are big chewers and puppies are indiscriminate in their choice of objects to put in their mouths. So, clear the room of any objects that you value. Take away all shoes, gloves, hats, anything in the room that could possibly find its way into your puppy's mouth. Remember, they will grow, and quickly, so the things you thought were out of reach at ten weeks soon won't be. You won't want to have rugs on the floor either for obvious reasons.

Hopefully that same room is large enough to have playtime there as well. Electrical outlets and electrical cords are another potential hazard. Remove the cords from Puppy's Place and make sure the electrical outlets are covered either with outlet covers or outlet plugs. You'll need to consider the electrical hazards in the rest of your house as you expand the dog's territory.

The Crate

Photo Courtesy of Nanc Schutte

I'm an advocate of crate-training from the get-go even if you don't intend to use it on a regular basis when your GSD is older. So, there should be a crate set up in Puppy's Place. You'll need a bed in the crate so that the little dog gets used to going in and out on his own to some extent. You want entering the crate to be a pleasure, not punishment. The crate should also be where some of his toys should initially be placed, although heaven knows they won't stay there very long.

It's important to have food and water bowls in Puppy's Place. When Cody was that age I started out with the food and water bowls in the crate just to get him going in and to associate the crate with a positive activity. I removed the bowls after feeding, although I did leave a water dish in the room so he could get a drink when desired. Mind you when Cody was a little bit older that also gave him an object to turn over and spill on the floor, but that goes with the puppy territory. Remember what I said about the floor. It will resemble a war zone for a while.

Some last thoughts about the crate. We bought a "large" crate with a divider so that we could make it half-size when the puppy was small and then expand it as the dog grew. Well, the "large" crate wasn't big enough so save yourself some expense and spring for the extra large at the very beginning. A full-grown dog should be able to stand up in her crate and turn around comfortably. Although I have a soft-sided crate for traveling, I don't recommend them for regular use. I have always used a wire crate in the house which has served us well.

A Mistake I Made

When we brought our German Shepherd puppy home, we put him in his crate that first night in Puppy's Place. I didn't realize it at the time but that is where I made a huge mistake. I thought I had it all figured out. I was going to get up every couple of hours and take him out to go potty. There was a lot of whining and crying. I mean a terrific amount, but I knew that was to be expected. This went on for many nights. More than it needed to. Only in retrospect did I find out, through trainers that I worked with and through my own reading, that the approach I had used was probably the worst thing I could have done. Remember, your puppy has just been taken from his family. He is in strange surroundings with people he doesn't know. It's not a good idea to put him in solitary and let him howl. Yes, you might be able to get a few winks but your dog is going to pay the price later.

Here's what you need to consider. Set up a second, much smaller crate (puppy size) either in your bedroom or just outside the bedroom door so your new GSP will know you are close. He'll be able to smell you. There still will be a nightly ruckus but that will gradually die down and then you can transition puppy to Puppy's Place for overnights eventually. Having the dog close by also helps understanding when he might have to go out to relieve himself. Believe me, it's a win-win situation. If a new puppy is left alone, especially at night, and especially when he first comes home, he will experience such intense anxiety that it may result in problematic behavior later on. So, bank on getting a little less sleep but having a healthier dog in the end. It's definitely worth it.

Household Hazards

The kitchen and perhaps the laundry room can be two of the biggest potential danger areas for your GSP. All those lower cupboards that may contain cleaning supplies, laundry soap, or even pest control poisons should be secured with childproof latches. Move anything like spices, candy, and baking supplies to an upper level so the temptation isn't there for the puppy. They will follow their noses and when they are that young what they find by smell ultimately goes into their mouths if possible. Garbage. Did I mention garbage? There's that smell thing again. Get in the habit of making sure your rubbish is bundled up and stored in a secure area. Just putting it outside isn't the solution.

You'll need to go through the rest of the house and be vigilant. In the bathrooms you'll need to make sure there is no access to things like

*Photo Courtesy of
Tricia Ansell*

medications, soaps, makeup, and personal hygiene products. In the living room, family room, and other common areas make sure there are no cell phone charger cords (or the phones themselves) available to be chomped on. Those small, plug-in flashlights should be removed from the electrical outlets. Pens, markers, scissors, and other sharp objects are also ingestion hazards. Breakable things like vases and artwork should be put well out of the way. Dogs can jump and don't always pay attention to where they are swinging their tails. Houseplants are easily knocked over, and in some cases consumed. Many household favorites are toxic to dogs. Here's a short list of common houseplants that you are better off without.

1. Aloe Plant

2. Jade

3. Cyclamen

4. Dracena

5. Many varieties of Lilies

6. Ficus Benjamina

7. Gardenia

8. Geranium

9. Schefflera

10. Oleander

Remember that's just the short list. As your German Shepherd puppy gets older and he shows less interest in botany it may be possible to bring some of your favorites back. Some dogs are deterred by a diluted lemon juice and water spray on the plant. At our house we found it was just simpler to say adios to the greenery for the duration.

Property Puppy Proofing

"Make sure your yard is secure with an 8 ft. fence with locks on all gates. It will only take them a couple of days to figure how to get out of the yard. Once they do, it will become an everyday thing."

Joyce Colburn
Hawaii German Shepherds

Just as you've had to alter your living arrangements inside, you need to take stock of your property and puppy-proof your great outdoors. Do you have a fenced-in yard with secure gate? Great, you are ahead of the game. Just do a double-check on the boarding to make sure it's secure and also check out areas where Flash might be able to make a getaway. Once they get a bit older, they can be habitual diggers so you might as well get used to deterring and safeguarding for that bad habit. At the same time, you might want to consider whether your fence is high enough. A six-foot fence is recommended because even the best-behaved dog can be tempted to leave the yard with the right enticement.

You'll need to put away stuff that you may have become accustomed to leave lying around. That includes all your gardening tools, including gloves. I don't know how much time I've wasted chasing Cody across the yard, the dog wearing a big smile with a glove firmly clenched in his mouth and the meaning of "drop" having completely flown out of his head. Once again, any chemicals like insecticides, dormant oil, and fertilizers need to be locked up. In a best-case scenario, the puppy might not consume any of that material but he sure can make a mess of the property and of himself. Lawn chair cushions won't last long if left lying around. If you have a pool you'll need to ensure that the puppy doesn't gain access. We have a fence around our pool and Cody has only recently been given freedom to stroll the pool area at the advanced age of four.

Something of very practical concern is choosing where your dog will do her business. Training her to go potty in a specific area will make cleanup a whole lot easier, and a lot less surprising.

Something of growing concern is the prevalence of ticks that carry Lyme disease. If you have a large property or a rural property it makes sense to keep as much of the grass that you can manage mowed on a regular basis. Ticks like to hang out in longer grass just waiting to attach themselves to anything passing by. These devious insects used to be primarily a rural problem but are now being found more often in urban areas. It's one more reason to keep a tidy yard.

Photo Courtesy of Makenzi Hall

Then there are some outdoor plants which are a problem for German Shepherds. The following list contains vegetation that is poisonous to dogs. For instance, a single bean from the Castor Bean plant is enough to prove fatal to a GSD.

1. Azalea

2. Daffodil

3. Tulip

4. Castor Bean

5. Foxglove

6. Lily of the Valley

7. Hosta

8. Morning Glory

9. Many Ivies

10. Clematis

One other plant I'll mention that is toxic to dogs is marijuana. At last count, medical marijuana is legal in twenty-nine states, and recreational marijuana is legal in nine states. It will probably only become more prevalent. Whether it is growing outdoors or sitting in a drawer or cupboard as an edible, it poses a threat to your German Shepherd. Remember, with her powerful nose she's going to know it's there. So, if you have marijuana in the house in any form, lock it away so your pup won't be able to get to it. If you grow it outside, how about roses instead? Your GSP will thank you for it.

Preparing Children and Other Pets

One of the best things you can do in advance of bringing your puppy home is to talk about the new routine everyone will have to get into. Like doggy chores. Who will feed her? How will she get her exercise? How about baths, and don't forget poop patrol. They can't all be glamorous jobs but everybody has to pitch in. I mean everyone wanted a puppy, right? The important thing to stress is, this isn't something you do for one day and if you don't like it you stop. This is the dog's forever home. That means you have to take care of her as long as she lives. Reminding everyone in the household that your German Shepherd puppy relies on them and that they are all responsible for keeping her safe is important.

If you already have another dog in the house, remember they have their routines and expectations, so it is important to maintain those when the new puppy comes home. You need to be sure to maintain the level of human attention for the first dog and make sure they continue to have their own space and things. When the pup comes home make sure they meet in some neutral territory, outside if the weather allows. The watchword here would be gradual. A little exposure at a time while the two dogs work things out. Don't tolerate any bad behavior but let the older dog take the lead and set the pace.

If there is a resident cat in your house you need to formulate a special introduction plan for Mr. GSP and the fearless feline. The key words in this scenario would be patience and more patience. At least in the beginning don't let them meet. Just let the animals get used to each other's smell being around. The first face-to-face should take place in an area where the puppy is on a leash and the kitty, while free to roam the room, cannot leave the area entirely. Variations of this process can be repeated until you see how the relationship is developing. They may learn to tolerate each other, they may become friends. That will be entirely up to them. You just have to give them a fair chance at working things out.

As this chapter draws to a close, I almost forgot a very important thing. You need to pick out the best name in the world for your dog. I'm partial to Axel and Jaeger if it's a male. Heidi or Zelda if it's a girl. I'm just saying.

Next up we'll talk about taking the big step. The day you bring your German Shepherd puppy home is going to be a time of high emotions, moving targets, and little sleep. Surviving the first few days with your sanity intact is all about being prepared and creating routines that everyone can anticipate and participate in. Did I mention you won't get much sleep?

CHAPTER 5
The Homecoming

The day we went to pick up our GSP, Cody, I had a lump in my throat all day. We had done our preparations throughout the house and I had read multiple books on puppy rearing but emotions were running high. So, I would suggest that will probably be the case with you too. Especially if children are involved. The one thing not to lose sight of is the plan you've made and talked about with all family members. In the excitement of your new GSP, everyone might be inclined to just wing it for the first few days. You need to be prepared to improvise a little bit when establishing life patterns and how your new puppy is going to fit into things, but if you forget everything else in those first few days remember this. You are beginning to establish life-long patterns for your puppy. Make sure you get off on the right foot.

Photo Courtesy of
Brent Ferguson

Before you leave the breeder's make sure you have several things in hand and several pieces of information in your head.

- The breeder should supply paperwork related to your puppy. This should include registration showing who the dam (mother) and sire (father) are. Also, your puppy may have been given an "official" name for registration purposes. You are not under any obligation to use that name for your dog in his real life. The breeder may also include your puppy's pedigree which shows his family tree.

- The breeder should also provide paperwork showing what shots the little guy has had and what deworming has been done. If there isn't a paper trail, make sure you get that information from the breeder and write it down yourself. You'll need that information when you go to the veterinarian for the first visit.

- Just a reminder, you should have had discussions with the breeder about any genetic diseases that have been associated with German Shepherds. At the very least you should understand from the breeder that your puppy's parents are clear of Dysplasia and DM (Degenerative Myelopathy). If there is paperwork confirming that, make sure you have a copy.

- Your breeder should supply a sample of the food your GSP has been eating so that there is no abrupt dietary change when you get her home. You can consult with your vet for the appropriate food choice later on.

- Another thing that will be comforting for your puppy is a small toy that has the scent of his mother and littermates on it. Also, a towel or small blanket with the smell of his mother is a good thing to have with you, not just for the ride home but for the first few weeks or longer. I still have the orange plush bone toy that Cody brought home with him that first day. He's five now and he still drags it out once in a while and sniffs it. Memories of home, I guess.

Homeward Bound

Time to hit the road. Make sure your puppy has had a chance to empty her tanks before getting in the car. Let her walk around a bit and do her business as much as possible. If you have a long ride ahead of you, there should be more stops along the way. Here's a crucial piece of information to remember. Until puppies have had their final vaccinations, they are susceptible to a variety of diseases. More about this later, but when you stop with your puppy on the way home, do it in less frequented areas and certainly where it is unlikely that other dogs will have relieved themselves. Hopefully you have family members with you so

*Photo Courtesy of
Laura Hernandez*

that one of them can hold the puppy on her lap for the ride home. You want to make the car ride as trauma free for your GSP as possible. Remember, there will be lots of car rides in the future and you want "going for a ride" to be fun, not punishment.

The First Night

"Expect a lot of whining and a tendency to back away from new and intimidating situations until the pup gets comfortable. The more they see within the first 14 weeks the better dog they become."

November Holley
Harrison K-9

Wow, you're home. There wasn't too much crying and whining on the way, was there? Now it's the first day of the rest of your lives. For your German Shepherd puppy, it's a whole new beginning, and she doesn't recognize any of her surroundings. Imagine, one minute you're with the pack and mom. The next minute you're with a bunch of strange humans. Pretty abrupt, don't you think? So, you need to cut your German Shepherd puppy a little slack here. And pack your patience. You'll need to have an abundance of that.

You know you have Puppy's Room set up but you probably need to do some initial socialization upon arrival. Especially if children are involved, they'll want to have some hands-on time. Just don't let anyone get too excited and above all don't get the puppy too revved up. Have a leash handy just in case you need to calm Tiger down a little bit. She is almost certainly to be chewy and nippy so keep some of her toys handy. When she starts to nip, distract her and divert her attention to a toy. Remembering to distract and divert is a lifelong approach that can be a lifesaver. I still have all my fingers and can attest to that.

Everyone sitting on the floor and letting little Heidi walk around with everyone touching her and talking to her is probably a good idea. It's a bonding moment. Not just for your GSD but it's the beginning of an emotional attachment for all family members. Believe it or not, even when your dog is grown up you will still look at her every once in a while and see the little puppy that she was. This is the beginning of loving your dog. No one has to teach that, you just have to let everyone do it. In their own way.

Bed Time

Puppies have many natural instincts. One of them is to howl and whine for attention. So, when it comes to bedtime that first night and for many nights after that, expect a routine ruckus. If you reflect back to the previous chapter, you'll remember that I suggested placing a small crate in your bedroom or close to the bedroom. Some dog owners that I've talked with say they put the crate near the bed and any time puppy was whining they would put their hand down near the dog so their smell would be strong and the puppy would know she wasn't alone. These first few days it's important to show your GSP that you are watching out for her and that you care. That will help with the gradual bonding process and ultimately create a healthy, happy dog.

Pet Supplies

It's not necessary to go out and buy everything you think your dog might ever need in his lifetime right off the bat. But it is important to have some essentials on hand when you bring your puppy home that are going to make life a little simpler. Make sure to have a supply of the food that the breeder was giving to your puppy. That will give you time, perhaps in consultation with your vet, to decide which diet is best for your dog. You need to read about the pros and cons of various diets and make some decisions.

Photo Courtesy of Tiffany Porter

Food and water bowls should be heavy enough that your puppy won't be able to flip them right away. That stage will come in time and you'll need to prepare for it, but sturdy, substantial bowls that will suffer hours of abuse will become part of the scenery. I don't feed Cody outside very often but I do have various bowls around the property for water so he can have a drink break depending on where we are. You may decide to have a set of outside bowls for your puppy if you spend a lot of time in the back yard, for instance.

We've talked about crates, but you may also want to purchase a child gate or two which will give you the ability to restrict your German Shepherd puppy to certain rooms. The one I use is metal with bars, a walk-through gate, and can be expanded to fit any door frame. It also has a locking latch on it that doesn't allow canine noses to flip it open.

Your GSP will need several collars. I keep a quick-drying one on hand that Cody wears when he goes to the beach. We also have sturdier ones that can be used with a leash. That's not to mention the various festive ones you might acquire along with those that have your favorite sports team logos on them. You'll soon find out that there are endless ways to spend money on your dog if you haven't already. The collars should have buckles so they can be resized as your puppy grows and also have metal rings to attach dog license tags, vaccination tags, and an identification tag. The ID tag should have your puppy's name, your name, and your phone number on it. You'll want to make sure the collars have snug fits but with a little give in them so that if, sorry not if, but when your GSP gets hung up on a bush or branch that it pulls off with a little effort.

Several leashes should also be in your inventory. There are many reasons not to purchase extendable or retractable leashes and certainly not for a large breed like a German Shepherd, so I'll be upfront about that. Don't waste your money on them. You should buy leather or nylon leashes in four- or six-foot lengths. No chain leashes. Too hard on the hands and perhaps dangerous for your dog.

And toys, lots of toys that will be chewed until they can't take it any more. We have a toy infirmary at our house where toys go to be rehabilitated if possible. Many unfortunately can't be saved so the toy budget is always in a state of flux and always running in the red. Toys that hide treats are also a great way for your dog to pass the time. My dog, Cody, has what we call his peanut butter bone. It's a rubber toy bone with holes in both ends where dabs of peanut butter can be placed so you can listen to a dog licking and smacking for twenty minutes or so.

Then there are grooming supplies. If you haven't seen the German Shedder jokes about how much GSDs shed you soon will. Brushes with

strong bristles are required for your dog's double coat. If you learn to clip your dog's nails, you'll save yourself a lot of cash so best to acquire a simple pair of scissor-type clippers. A few other items on your to-buy list:

- Lots of plastic poop bags
- Poop-scooper
- Cleaning supplies (make sure whatever you use is puppy safe)

Vet Visits

You need to form a relationship with a reliable veterinarian very early on. Your breeder may even have stipulated that the puppy needs to see a vet shortly after arriving in your home. That actually protects the breeder and you. If the puppy is unhealthy you'll find out right away. Then you and your breeder can decide a course of action. Responsible breeders will take unhealthy pups back and refund your money, or work with you to achieve satisfaction. The longer the puppy is with you the more emotional attachment there is. No matter what, an early vet visit should definitely be in the cards.

There are various ways to decide which vet is best for you. Proximity is certainly a consideration, but word of mouth reputation is probably one of the best ways of helping you decide. Once you have a name or two that you are considering, pay a visit and ask some questions. While you're there check out how clean the premises seem to be. I always pay attention to staff attitude. If they make you feel welcome and genuinely seem to care, then that goes a long way. Take the time to chat with a client or two about their experiences and how long they've been coming to the location. Busy clinics can be a sign of customer satisfaction so don't be put off by client volume. The hours of operation are a major consideration and if they offer emergency services that's a large bonus. There will be at least one or two "emergency" visits in your pet's career so if you know the people and can get there in a hurry everyone is going to feel better about that.

Hands On

The first veterinarian visit will be a learning experience for everyone involved. Your puppy gets a first taste of the outside world and quite possibly other dogs (and cats) in the vet's office. You will get to see how you need to deal with your German Shepherd puppy in terms of aggressiveness or timidity. Some puppies just barrel out into the world and accept whatever comes their way. Other, less extroverted dogs may have to be coaxed into things.

One of the tips I learned early on was not to encourage fear or worry, especially as puppies mature. If a puppy is concerned about something and exhibiting how worried she is, it's not a good idea to pet the dog and try to reassure it. If you do that, inadvertently you are sending signals to your dog that it is OK to be worried and even to react badly. Once again, the best thing to do is to "distract and divert." That could be with a favorite toy or a treat. Just as with a young child, if you occupy the puppy's mind with another experience, they forget to be worried.

This initial visit is like many first things in your German Shepherd puppy's early life. If the experience is fun and there is little to no pain involved, your puppy will not have any bad associations with the vet visit. I have seen adult dogs being dragged or carried, kicking and screaming, into the vet office. You don't want to be one of those owners trying to coax an eighty-five-pound GSD through the office door. It's really hard on you and your dog so do everything you can to steer the process in the right direction from the beginning. You'll save a lifetime of worry and fear for both you and, more importantly, your German Shepherd.

The Nitty Gritty

Another tip to remember. Your GSP is too young to have full immunity in order to resist many of the diseases that are lurking out there. Most vet offices do a pretty good job of making sure the floor area is clean but as they say, "poop happens." Accidents will have occurred so make sure you carry your pup into the office and keep her in your lap until you're in the examination room. Better safe than sorry.

The vet will go through a routine checklist with your puppy. He is looking to establish the general health of your dog and also to see if there are any outward signs of congenital defects. Your vet is your partner in the care of your dog, so I always try to remember that they are a friend and are just trying to help. Here is what will happen during that first examination.

- Your GSP's eyes and ears will be inspected.

- Teeth, tongue, gums, and throat will get some scrutiny. Pinkness should be the order of the day. Black spots may be present which are nothing to worry about.

- Your vet will get a stethoscope out and listen to your puppy's heart and also check on her lungs to make sure the breathing is effortless and lungs are clear.

- Your puppy will be weighed on this and every subsequent visit. A dog's weight is a very good indicator of health. Too heavy or too thin and a different diet could be recommended.

- The vet will do a lot of touching and feeling around, especially in your puppy's abdominal area. He is looking for any signs of sensitivity which could indicate a problem. Toes, toenails, paws, and anal area will be checked out.

- Your puppy will be scrutinized as she walks around to make sure the gait is normal with no signs of limping or soreness.

- During the examination ask all the questions you can think of. Remember, you have an expert at your disposal so take advantage of the time. Make sure you provide the vet with any paperwork or information regarding your German Shepherd puppy that the breeder may have given you.

- Depending on the age of the pup, vaccinations may be required. These don't really hurt your dog but you may want to provide a treat or a toy to be chewed on when the needle is being wielded.

After the examination is over make sure you are scheduled for the additional shots that your puppy requires. There are a series of recommended vaccines as well as optional or "non-core" shots. One optional one to consider if you might be boarding your dog at any point is the Bordetella, or "kennel cough" vaccine. Many kennels have this as a requirement before accepting your dog.

Training the Tyke

"Something that most people don't seem to realize is that you can start training from day one. They are smart, and they will surprise you with how much they can learn right out of the gate. This is a crucial time to start laying the foundations for behaviors you want to see in them as adults."

Celeste Schmidt
Dakonic German Shepherds

Training with your GSD isn't an option. It's a necessity. Dogs don't suddenly become socially well-mannered and obedient overnight and through osmosis. You have to spend time with them, either one-on-one or in group classes. Both are beneficial. If you are lucky enough to have a number of organizations offering group instruction, one of the things to take into account would be to inquire if they offer classes specifically for large breeds. That way you might avoid the uncomfortable group class situation that I described in Chapter Three.

Puppy Class

Your puppy's first exposure to his peers should probably be through a puppy class. This group togetherness is as much about socialization as it is training but it is definitely worthwhile. Most dog people will agree that the first four months of your German Shepherd puppy's life is the time when they are most impressionable. So, it's the ideal time to begin his education. Puppy classes can deal with everything from some of the issues you're working on at home like potty training and crate-training tips to familiarizing Fritz with people in uniform. Your GSP will also just be spending time around other puppies, which is invaluable. It's a good experience for you as well. You get to talk with other owners and share stories and tips. Maybe you also get to laugh a little bit too. Dog socializing and training sometimes seems to be overwhelmingly serious. Learn to lighten up a little bit and you will feel refreshed and recharged, ready to tackle the next lesson.

Medical tip:
> During this time in your puppy's life, while he is being vaccinated and acquiring his full immunity, it's important to limit his exposure to places and other animals that might pass something along to him. Make sure that the organization offering the puppy classes you attend requires all the dogs to be participating in a vaccination program. The class organizers should have a strict hygiene protocol that requires thorough cleaning of areas in group class use. For those first few months of your puppy's life the benefits of socialization outweigh the minimal risks of infection in the big wide world.

Breaking the Bank?

Photo Courtesy of Hannah Wynd

Hopefully the first-year expenses associated with your new best friend won't break the bank, but you do need to cobble together some sort of general budget. Remember you can spend as much as you want to, but there is a minimum amount that is going to be essential. The ASPCA estimates that a large breed puppy's first year will set you back on average more than eighteen hundred dollars, which doesn't include the initial purchase cost. Let's break down some of those costs.

Initial Purchase Cost of Puppy

If you are buying a purebred GSP in the United States the amount you pay will vary. Also, what you intend to do with your puppy will impact the price. If you're looking for a high-drive dog that should excel in obedience and protection, you could part with five thousand dollars or more.

Looking for a family dog and personal companion? That price tag would likely start at a more moderate thousand dollars and go up from there.

Vet/Medical Costs

The American Pet Products Association estimates that pet owners in the U.S. spent more than sixteen billion dollars on vet care in 2017. That sounds like a stunning amount and it is, but remember the sophistication of technology and medicines in the pet world has kept pace with its human counterpart. Here are a few examples of what individual costs might look like.

- The basic charge for a vet visit starts at about fifty dollars. If you add vaccinations that can add twenty dollars per shot.

- Spay/neuter costs of two hundred dollars or more are not uncommon.

- Larger dogs like German Shepherds will cost more to treat because more medication is needed, for example.

- An emergency vet visit charge can average more than a hundred dollars. That doesn't include things like bloodwork and X-rays. Add several hundred dollars for those procedures. If your dog needs emergency surgery, that can run in the thousands of dollars.

I think you get the picture and it does make pet insurance look very attractive.

Pet Insurance

The premiums on pet insurance will vary depending on the age of your dog at enrollment, your deductible, and the medical services covered by the type of insurance you purchase. The range you are looking at would generally be monthly premiums ranging from twenty-five to seventy dollars.

Food and Treats

All the costs I'm detailing will vary, and so it is with food and treats. If your dog is basically a dry kibble eater (I personally don't know too many of those) your food budget will be pretty basic. If you start throwing in some canned, wet food the costs start to creep up. If you feed your dog a raw diet, that can be very expensive unless you process most of the meat yourself. Let's average out your food bill starting at about seventy dollars a month.

Crates & Basics

Expect to spend one hundred dollars or more on an extra-large crate. Good-quality collars will be twenty dollars. You might as well buy sturdy leashes to begin with because you will have an eighty-pound dog on the other end eventually, so set aside thirty dollars per leash in your budget. The walk-through pet gate that I use is about forty dollars.

Toys

You have total discretion here. Cody has always enjoyed chewing and tearing up sticks or branches and here in the country those are free. But he also has a lot of squeaker toys and balls. Each of those can cost eight dollars so they add up in a hurry. I also found with a younger dog I bought more toys. Now with a "mature" GSD I buy fewer, but better-quality toys. If they survive the first couple of days, I know they'll be around for a while.

Training

Group classes will be the most affordable but will still cost in the one-hundred-fifty-dollar range for a six-week session. If you continue into specialized training, expect to spend three thousand dollars for a personal protection course as an example.

Grooming

You can do much of the grooming yourself. If you keep it up on a daily and weekly basis then visits to a groomer need not take place. Remember, GSDs don't need frequent baths unless they get absolutely filthy or encounter a skunk. The nails you can clip at home. My dog, Cody, gets brushed out every night so never gets into a tangled mess which his plush coat would tend to do. If you do go to a groomer, you could pay as much as ninety dollars a session if you go infrequently. Don't forget to brush your dog's teeth. They love peanut-butter-flavored toothpaste.

Daycare/Dog Walking

Doggy daycare can cost about forty dollars a day. For dog walking you're probably looking at about twenty dollars per trot.

We've arrived at the stage where your dog will begin to grow like a weed physically. A mental maturation process is taking place as well. As a responsible owner you need to stay on top of your evolving German Shepherd in order to make sure she becomes the sociable, responsible, obedient dog she needs to be. Now is when you need to invest time early on in dealing with many of the annoying habits like chewing and digging that can get out of hand if you don't curb them now.

I remember that my German Shepherd, Cody, as a puppy had an annoying habit of picking up stones and chewing on them. I had to make a point of watching him and every time he picked a rock up, I would take it away from him and tell him no. I had dreams about Cody chewing rocks. If I was out for a walk with my wife and the dog, I would always be saying to her, "Did he just pick up a stone?" If my puppy could be persistent in chewing on rocks, I could be just as persistent in taking them away from him. Yes, the behavior can last for months but you can win in the end. Let's look at some of those things you'll need to deal with early on so you don't have a canine juvenile delinquent later on in life.

CHAPTER 6
Being a Proud Puppy Parent

Photo Courtesy of Morgan Hill

Let me start this chapter with a personal tale. My German Shepherd, Cody, has never been motivated by treats. I figured that out early on in my career as a dog dad. So, I had to decipher what motivated him to do things that I wanted him to do, but that he mostly had little to zero interest in accomplishing. As a puppy, one of the first things I wanted Cody to learn was to come to me when I called him. Trainers call it "recall" or, depending on how well it's performed, "solid recall." Sounds simple enough, but try telling a twelve-week-old toddler who only wants to sniff things and put rocks in his mouth that he should come when asked. As the days went by with minimal to no success, I discovered that he liked chasing me and certainly loved being chased. So, I would say "Come" and run away from him and when he caught me, I would always pet him and tell him what a good boy he was. For Cody it was, and still is, all about the game and the positive reinforcement that he gets when doing something that I ask him to.

That's my long-winded way of telling you that in your career as a puppy parent, your focus should be on positive reinforcement of your German Shepherd's behavior. Negative reinforcement, or punishment, only teaches your dog to modify behavior out of fear. I don't know anyone who enjoys seeing a fearful dog, cowering because of a misstep. Life's too short. So positive reinforcement should be the foundation of everything you and your dog accomplish. It won't be easy. And remember, if you want to shout at someone, go find a mirror.

Crate Controversy

Go onto any German Shepherd dog group on Facebook or other social media and ask whether you should crate-train your GSD, and then stand back. There will be a thundering avalanche of pro-craters and an equal barrage of anti-craters. People who don't support crate-training will say that confinement is cruel and they will never allow their dogs to be locked up in a cage. Those who support using a crate say that crate-training is just a tool and that it in fact can give a dog a sense of security.

This is where the concept of positive reinforcement begins to play itself out in your home. Crate training shouldn't be abused. It's not meant as punishment. It is meant as a personal space for your GSD, as a refuge if she has had enough and wants to get away from it all. One of the major arguments against crate use is that it isn't good for your GSD to be locked away for sixteen hours a day. And I agree with that. It should never be used as a substitute for a dog walker or doggy day care or even you getting off the sofa and getting some of those ten thousand steps that we are all supposed to walk every day to be healthy. It can be used for several hours during the day when you have to be away and you want your dog to be safe. Cody sleeps in his crate at night and goes into it willingly at about seven o'clock every evening. Sometimes I find him hanging out there at other times, especially after lunch when he is taking a siesta. That's his habit and he's happy with it. You need to figure out your routine and stick with it.

Photo Courtesy of Celeste Schmidt Dakonic GSDs

So, here's what I suggest. Crate-train your puppy. It will be useful for her, and you, while she is going through some of the more destructive, youthful stages. Decide as your GSP gets older whether continuing to use a crate makes sense for your lifestyle or not. Then get on with your life. The sky isn't going to fall if you do or don't crate-train. But while we're talking about crates, let's go through some of the basics on how to get the most out of what is, after all, just one option in your arsenal of training tools.

*Photo Courtesy of
William Chilton*

Crate Culture

All dogs want to learn. Some are smarter than others, that's true, and it may be a longer educational curve for some dogs, but ultimately, they all want to do the right thing, to please you, and be happy. German Shepherd puppies are light years from being responsible though. They are governed by their senses, their appetites, and an insatiable curiosity. That little puppy package that I've just described is what can get them into trouble. Sometimes serious trouble that can hurt them, so it's up to you to be responsible because they can't be, right now. One of those ways of fulfilling your obligations is to monitor and control your puppy's behavior.

The First Few Weeks

You and your puppy have begun to know each other. One of the important things to have been exposing your pup to is having him spend time in his crate. His food and water bowls should be in there so at chow time he goes in there voluntarily. I wouldn't leave the bowls in the crate at other times. Put his toys in his crate so that he has to go in to get them. Don't shut the door on him so he doesn't think that every time he goes inside he's going to be locked in. His daytime bed should be in there. Treats should be dispensed in the crate. You need to create the impression that all good things revolve around the crate. At night he should be in the bedroom crate so that he begins to understand that routine and knows what is expected of him. We'll delve more into the usefulness of this tool but suffice it to say, crates can play a large role in potty training as well. GSDs are incredibly smart and catch on to most things very quickly. If they aren't giving you the desired behavior it's because you haven't found the right key to unlock it.

Chewing & Biting

Nipping and mouthing is probably the single most common complaint from GSD owners. It starts very young and if left unchecked will stretch right into adulthood. German Shepherds explore things with their mouths. They placate themselves by chewing on things. Toys, shoes, baseboards, rugs, you name it, these dogs are all geniuses when it comes to taking things apart. Check out the survival strategies I've outlined in the following section on teething.

Teething

One of the reasons your GSP chews is teething. Your puppy has twenty-eight baby teeth, but it sure feels like more sometimes. He will start to lose those sharp dentures starting at twelve weeks old or so. Therein lies the problem. Puppies like to chew naturally but when teething is in full swing, it takes things to a whole new level. Baby teeth falling out, adult teeth slowly coming in, is a recipe for bad behavior on your GSP's part, and frustration on yours. That said, there are some strategies for coping.

a) Desperate Strategy #1

Divert and distract. When your puppy bites, tell him no and make a big show of giving him a favorite toy to play with. Change his mind. I know I've mentioned it before, but it does work.

b) Desperate Strategy #2

If your pup bites, say "ouch" loudly and step away from him. Stop any play that might have been going on. The theory is that your little genius will associate biting with play time being taken away and therefore he will self-correct. That's the theory anyway.

c) Desperate Strategy #3

This is a technique that I used on Cody and his puppy brain seemed to pick up on it quite quickly. When he would bite me, I would of course say no maybe with an "ouch" first. Then I would put my hand in his mouth with my thumb under his tongue and my index finger under his chin. Because this makes the dog uncomfortable, they'll struggle to get away from you. It doesn't hurt the puppy and they soon learn that if they chew on you, you will lean on them. Like I said, they are smart little creatures.

Growling & Barking

Something to keep in mind is that all puppies growl, bark, and bite. It's in their nature, it's how they play with each other, it's how they want to play with you, it's normal behavior. You should know your German Shepherd puppy well enough after a few days to tell the difference between playing and plain aggressiveness. Most puppies' bodies are fairly relaxed when in play mode but if you notice some tension it's time to stop. Stop the game, remove yourself if you need to, and allow your puppy time to reset. He wants your time and attention more than anything so he should pick up on the cues quickly.

Digging and Digging and Digging

Why do puppies dig? Primarily your German Shepherd puppy is going to dig for entertainment because she is bored. Here is the best way to deal with that behavior.

- Exercise. While it is important not to stress out a puppy's body by physically over-exercising her, you need to give her the opportunity to burn off all that youthful energy. Lots of short walks, playing with toys, even basic games of fetch will help tire your GSP out. Practicing commands will exhaust everyone involved, so five minutes of that at a time and no one will have any energy for anything.

There are several other motivations for tearing up the backyard. Some older pups are looking for a change in scenery. Not that the hospitality isn't great at your house, it's just that there is a whole wide world out there to be discovered. That may be why Zelda is trying to make a break for it by attempting to dig under the fence or by a foundation wall. Here are some approaches to help deal with the escape artist.

- First of all, monitor your puppy while in the back yard. If you're just turning her loose out there and then leaving for the day then you

60

take what you get. That should never be the case. While watching her, if you see digging behavior you can take steps to stop it. Go out and say no and preoccupy her with some activity for a couple of minutes that will change the dog's mindset.

- You can install some physical barriers that will prevent digging under a fence such as chain-link fencing anchored to the ground.

Here is my if-all-else-fails suggestion. Some German Shepherds, no matter how much you try to change their behavior, once in a while still fall back on old, bad habits. Maybe they had a stressful day at the dog park or their evening bowl of kibble wasn't quite up to snuff. They may not even know the reason but before you know it the dirt is flying. If your back is against the wall, try this.

- Set aside an area where digging IS allowed. I know, sounds counter-intuitive, right? Well no, not really. Digging becomes a reward, a controlled behavior. You can take them to the area and praise them. Special toys could be buried treasures for Zelda to discover. If digging commences in another area, stop that activity immediately and proceed to the open pit mine location.

Sometimes it's just as important to know how not to proceed. Socializing and training a German Shepherd takes time and there are very few shortcuts. I want to end this section with several things I do not recommend when dealing with a digging dog.

Photo Courtesy of Autumn Raines

- In line with the positive reinforcement approach, no electric fences. It really is a punishment in order to facilitate a change. Shocking a dog when she approaches a barrier can cure one behavior while potentially creating several other problems.

- Don't use hot pepper sprays or other concoctions that might harm your puppy and other animals. Put the time in to help your German Shepherd, not hurt her.

- Never punish your dog for digging. Correct the behavior as soon as you see it happening so the puppy associates the admonishment with something unacceptable.

One last note. Cody, at the ripe old age of five, still has one spot that he likes to go to and dig. It happens to be in a flower bed right by the front door. He's never been devious about where he digs, it's just that one spot that seems to be irresistible to him. If he sees me watching him, he stops and pretends he was just inspecting things. Old habits die hard. Can you dig it?

Separation Anxiety

HELPFUL TIP
Microchipping Your Dog

Having your dog microchipped is quick, affordable, and a great way to make sure a runaway pet makes it safely home. German Shepherds are extremely intelligent and may surprise you by finding creative ways to leave your property. Talk to your veterinarian or local animal shelter about chip recommendations. Always make sure to update your microchip with current contact information, and don't skip the collar and tags!

Separation anxiety is more common than you think, and it can develop early in your puppy's life. Veterinarians at the University of Illinois suggest that as many as forty percent of the nation's dogs may experience a form of separation anxiety. Dogs bond with their owners quickly. Remember you're the source of all good food and experiences. You're their gateway to fun. When you leave the house without them, some dogs, especially rescues, can feel abandoned. They are fearful that you're never coming back. Here are some circumstances that can prompt SA.

- Your schedule changes suddenly with no attempt to transition to the revised hours.
- Moving to a new location.
- A family member they are attached to suddenly disappears. It could be someone going away to school or sadly a death in the family.
- Some dogs need to be re-homed through no fault of their own and that can cause anxiety.

You may not realize that your change in circumstance has triggered an emotional problem in your German Shepherd until he starts to act out. None of the behavior the SA-prone dog exhibits can be considered intentional, meaning they aren't doing it to spite you or get back at you for leaving them. They are genuinely terrified and how they behave is a reflex reaction to fear. Your puppy may show some of the following be-haviors if separation anxiety is becoming a problem.

- If you have been crate-training your puppy he may attempt to es-cape. Some dogs are strong enough to bend wire crates and get out. Some dogs can only bend the metal enough to get themselves into trouble. You may have to stop using the crate and use baby gates to confine your GSD to an appropriate room.

- Destruction of household items. A puppy experiencing SA may chew on doorframes or baseboards, chairs, table legs, rugs, anything that is in his room. As with the crate destruction your German Shepherd may hurt themselves during their bout of anxiety.

- Urination and defecation.

- Pacing and barking.

All of these behaviors may be signs of SA but if your GSD does any of these things a visit to the veterinarian is probably in order. You need to rule out any medical problems in your animal.

Quick Tips on Dealing with Separation Anxiety

SA can be a complex challenge to deal with because there are indi-vidual, complicated little personalities lurking in those canine craniums. If you find your GSD is exhibiting symptoms, here are a couple of gener-al solutions to think about. You'll have to do more of your own research, and you may have to seek professional help. There is one thing you can be sure of. It won't go away on its own and your dog won't grow out of it.

- Just as your puppy has been unconsciously conditioned to fret when you aren't there, he can be conditioned to relax. One of the crucial things to keep in mind is the negative-positive balance. If you grad-ually turn the negative into a positive, a change in behavior should result. Dogs that are motivated by favorite foods are the easiest to help in this way. Toys left with favorite treats in them can help ease anxiety when you are gone. Short trips out and then back can help your GSD understand that you always return.

- For cases of severe anxiety, you should seek a qualified dog trainer, or, if you are lucky enough to live in an area where you have animal behavior specialists, seek one out.

Home Alone

Photo Courtesy of
Patti Baxter - Jasper

Separation anxiety aside, you should be working on gradually leaving your puppy alone for periods of time. All dogs need to learn to be by themselves because they will have to cope with some solitude throughout their lifetimes. Starting off with short absences is the best way to begin. Leaving a light on and the radio playing or some soft music in the background helps make up for human absence.

I know that when I was at this stage with Cody, I would put him in his crate, obviously getting ready to leave with my stomping around, and then slam the door loudly on my way out. Then I would stand there and listen. The first few times there was silence initially, and then I would hear small barks, gaining slowly in volume. After a minute or two of this, but not so much that Cody was completely wound up, I would open the door and stomp back in. The barking would immediately cease. Then I would walk around the house where he could see me and I would leave again. I would mix the days up with some short-term departures and then longer absences. Sometimes when I would return home and if there was barking, I would walk in, look at Cody in his crate, say "no barking," and then let him out and we would carry on. It was several weeks of this kind of operation before I returned home one day, and not only was there no barking, but the only sound coming out of the crate was snoring.

Here are some other thoughts to ponder as you go through the "Home Alone" process.

1. Start the process as early as possible. The sooner your German Shepherd puppy grasps the routine and realizes that you do actually come home every time you leave, the happier everyone will be.

2. In the buildup to some absences, make sure to pointedly ignore your GSP sometimes. He needs to know that you aren't going to amuse him twenty-four hours a day. That for some of the time during the day he will be left with his puppy thoughts and his toys for entertainment.

3. When you do leave, especially if you aren't using a crate, no long emotional goodbyes. You don't want to give the puppy cues telling him it's time to get anxious. Coming and going without any fanfare is the way to proceed. I know it's hard on the ego but you'll get over it.

4. I know we've talked about exercise, but it really is a key to many things. Make sure your puppy has had lots of activity combined with some cool-down time before you go out. If your pup is suitably exhausted before your departure, they may just sleep the whole time you're away.

Bedtime for Beasty Boy

German Shepherd puppies sleep a tremendous amount. You will soon see a rhythm to little Fritz's existence. Sleep, eat, pee and/or poop, play, sleep, pee and/or poop, and the cycle carries on. Puppy should be sleeping in his crate in order to have a continuing positive association with the wire contraption. Here's a checklist you can use to make sure bedtime is quiet time.

- ✔ Let your GSP sleep as much as he wants to.
- ✔ Make sure your puppy gets plenty of exercise during the day so he will be tired in the evening.
- ✔ Make sure he has had a potty trip before hitting the sack.
- ✔ No frenetic activity for at least an hour before bedtime.
- ✔ Bedtime should be approximately the same time every night, so the routine that all German Shepherds love gets established early.
- ✔ His sleeping crate should be comfortable enough that you might think about crawling in for a nap.
- ✔ Don't forget puppies are chewing machines. A toy should be in his crate so he can satisfy that need.

We have covered quite a bit of territory in this chapter, but really only the bare foundation has been laid for a successful partnership between you and your German Shepherd. In the next chapter we'll go into some depth on how you can keep your beautiful home in one piece, more or less, AND still love your GSD. It can be done.

CHAPTER 7
Housetraining

"The biggest thing with house training is to get on a schedule and be ready. If puppy wakes up from a nap, take them out, puppy gets done playing, take them out, etc, etc. Also be aware of water intake, if puppy is peeing constantly you might want to control the water intake a bit more. Picking it up a couple hours before bed time is usually for the best as well."

Celeste Schmidt
Dakonic German Shepherds

Toilet training, potty training, call it what you will, the goal is to make sure your German Shepherd puppy learns to urinate and defecate in the approved area and that they gradually learn to hold it until the approved spot is available to them. The key to this is understanding that there is a puppy equation you can work with and it sure takes a lot of the guesswork out of the poo process. As the old saying goes, timing is every-

Photo Courtesy of
Maria Stylianou

thing, and that is never more applicable than when it comes to a young dog pooping and peeing. Pups can hold things one hour for every month they have been around. When your GSP comes home at eight weeks they are good for two hours, more or less. After that it's a crap shoot. When those one hundred twenty minutes have elapsed, every additional second is a window of opportunity for your furry rascal. Potty training will be one of the most tedious training tasks you will have to go through with your little home wrecker but when they "get it" and start to let you know that they know, then your sighs of relief will be heard blocks away. Let's tackle some of the basic methods of making your puppy understand that doing his business is an outside job, not an inside joke.

Perfecting Potty Performance

Remember that crate-training controversy we talked about earlier? Well, I'm going to bring it back for another quick go-round. Using a crate when potty training makes a whole lot of sense, for a couple of reasons.

> ➢ Memories of mama. The mother dog keeps the litter area clean even though there are six or seven or eight pups strolling around making a mess. Gradually the puppies get the picture and they then go further afield to do their business. The idea of keeping the immediate living area clean is imprinted in them early by that authority figure above all authority figures, mom. The pups carry that personal hygiene gem with them the rest of their lives.

HELPFUL TIP
Enzyme Solution

House-training dogs can be a messy business. The first line of defense for cleaning up a puppy accident should always be to blot the area immediately, soaking up as much liquid as possible. But for fighting stubborn puppy accident stains and odors, consider using a pet-safe enzyme cleaner. Bio-enzymatic cleaners use good bacteria to break down odor-causing molecules, such as ammonia, to eliminate smells and remove stains. Removing the smell of an accident can even help prevent your pet from becoming confused about the location of the bathroom and therefore prevent further accidents.

➢ Custom crating. First of all, you can purchase crates in different sizes, which helps with giving your puppy enough space when inside, but not too much so that he can saunter to the back forty, potty, and then stroll back to his fun zone. Crates also come with dividers so you can buy a larger size to accommodate future growth but use the divider to make the immediate living space consistent with your pup's current physical size.

If you would feel better about using a puppy playpen instead of a crate, it can work very well, especially while your German Shepherd puppy is relatively young. All of the same techniques mentioned for crate-training are applicable to the playpen with less overhead. That's a little attempt at humor there but my research tells me that depending on the playpen, they are somewhat less expensive than crates.

Leaving the crate concept behind for a minute, let's examine some of the other things that will help you get ahead of the potty parade. You know that a puppy can only hold her urine and feces for a limited time because of her age. That is underlying principle number one, so let's build on that. It is never too early to establish routines with your German Shepherd puppy. Combine bodily functions with routine and here's another equation that will help indicate when your youngster will have to go out to potty.

The Potty Predictor
- First thing in the morning
- After eating and/or drinking
- After playing
- After enjoying some crate time
- After a nap
- Last thing at night

You can take potty practice to the extreme. I know because I was guilty of it with my German Shepherd, Cody. When he was eight and nine weeks old, and because I knew that he could only hold it for a couple of hours at that age, I used to set my alarm throughout the night and get up every two hours to take Cody out. Well, the little puppy would be in a sound sleep, after crying himself into a state of exhaustion, and I would wake him up to stagger outside and stare at the stars. Sometimes he went potty, sometimes he was asleep on his puppy paws. I probably didn't need to be quite that obsessive. I was being a helicopter parent but I didn't know any better. I do now and so do you.

Those potty predictors I mentioned are just some of the times to be aware of. You should be spending a fair amount of time observing your GSP; her physical behavior will also give you some clues when it's time to head for the potty door. If you're not watching her, accidents will happen and they're your fault, not your puppy's mistake. You are the one with the great big human brain with all those neural networks that allow you to anticipate the future. Well, for you, the future is right now and she's walking around on four feet looking for a place to go potty.

Physical Potty Pointers

- Sniffing. This means your puppy is on the hunt and you don't need two guesses what for. Out the door you go.

- Circling and general restlessness. Doggy distress means a mess can't be far behind.

- Puppy pause. GSPs may suddenly freeze right in the middle of an activity they're involved in. If this happens it's time to make a beeline.

- Sitting or whining at the door. If this happens you are on your way to potty nirvana. Your little German Shepherd is getting the idea. Out the door and lots of praise. You might even want to go inside and have a celebratory drink.

Potty Lingo

Here's something else to think about that might just make your life easier and save a few minutes of valuable time. I guess I would describe it as your personal poo command. Pick a phrase that you'll be able to use anywhere, anytime, without undue embarrassment. It could be as simple as "go potty." Remember, commands need to be short. Every time you take your German Shepherd puppy out to do his business be ready and poised with your personal poo command. Initially the little guy won't have a clue as to what it means but every time he pees or poos, you repeat the command. Gradually you introduce the command prior to the dog's bodily function happening. Eventually, with some persistence, the two of you should be on the same woo-woo wavelength and mission accomplished can take minutes instead of hours. It will cut down on Fritz's sniffing and stargazing time but he'll get over it.

Puppy Room Revisited

Remember our old linoleum floor that I mentioned in Chapter Four? There were a fair amount of potty "accidents" in that room. We used newspaper in the Puppy Room initially to get our eight-week-old to potty in certain areas. Paper training, like every method, has its advocates and its detractors. Cody, obviously a non-believer, initially would pee on the linoleum floor and then go over and tear up the newspaper. That's not how the paper system is supposed to work. I'll cover this system briefly because for German Shepherds I don't believe it should be used except as a brief transition phase to doing business outside. If you have a Jack Russell then perhaps today's headlines could be more of a help.

Building a Paper Case

Photo Courtesy of Eduardo De Luna

The idea of putting newspaper (or puppy pads) down is to get your GSP to potty on the papered area. Then you gradually reduce the covered area, eventually leaving just the paper closest to the door that leads to the outside and then no paper at all. I would use this technique only in the initial stages of training and in emergency circumstances where you are called away and can't watch your puppy. You will know that leaving a very young dog in a crate for a length of time is NOT something to contemplate. So perhaps, paper it is, at least initially.

Opening Doors

While some folks may believe that doggy doors are most suitable for small dogs, German Shepherds can use them as well. When it comes to potty training, they can be a time saver if your house is configured the right way; not only saving time, but if you have to leave your puppy home unmonitored, then if he has been housetrained properly, you won't have to worry about him messing up. Every time your puppy has to go potty you have been taking

Photo Courtesy of Nicole Mckenzie

him out the same door, right? Each time, the same door, the same routine. Dogs thrive on knowing the rules and understanding what is going to happen. If you have a doggy door, the rule is to take Junior out that way to go potty so that it becomes just the thing you do.

When you are ready to see if your puppy can manage on his own, initially you'll need to make sure that the inside living space your puppy is confined in is relatively small. You'll want it all to remind him of Memories of Mama. He won't want to use his inside space to relieve himself so out he goes through the doggy door. Your outside space will have to be secure so Junior can't get into any trouble while he's on a potty run. A doggy door might just open some doors for you in working out the potty puzzle.

The Time Frame

One of the unanswered questions of this chapter is, how long is this whole process going to take? How many days, weeks, months am I going to be watching this little genius for signs that she has to go outside to the potty zone? When can I finally get some sleep, when will this be over? To be honest, it's an open-ended question. GSDs are extremely smart so if it's taking a long time and you're wondering why, better haul the old mirror out again. Four months should be an outside ballpark estimate, but many dogs are well on their way to being housetrained before then. With that good news under your belt let's get ready for the next chapter. It's all about your German Shepherd and the outside world. They don't automatically know how to behave in every situation, and they will look to you for cues and clues to what their behavior should be. Let's call it the social animal chapter.

CHAPTER 8
The Social Animal

"Get your new GSD puppy out and around people and dogs as soon as your vet says it's safe to do so."

Tracy Berg
vom Haus Berg German Shepherds

Photo Courtesy of Patti Baxter - Jasper

Socialization. Why would we have to think about that in relation to our German Shepherd puppies? Don't we just roll with the punches, let the chips fall where they may and take one day at a time? The short answer is no. Canine behavior can be extremely unpredictable UNLESS you have made the effort to mold and expose your GSP to the varied social possibilities and responsibilities in the big, wide world.

I knew one of my biggest challenges when we brought our GSD home would be socialization because we live on a rural property. There are no other dogs to expose Cody to, few people come by during the course of a week, and short of the odd squirrel, rabbit, or coyote, Cody is stuck gazing into my bloodshot, brown eyes most of the time. So, I have had to make a point of taking him places with me in the truck, making the forty-five-minute drive to the nearest dog park, taking one-on-one lessons with a trainer, and generally exposing him to whatever the day has to offer. Does the occasional service repairman have to put up with Cody nuzzling him, trying to coax a throw of a tattered Frisbee or a kick of a deflated basketball down the hill for the dog to chase? Sure, but If I hadn't made those socialization efforts, I would in all likelihood have a fearful, insecure, and potentially dangerous eighty-five-pound dog that would only perpetuate the false stereotype of the aggressive, out of control German Shepherd. I didn't want that and neither do you.

– Photo Courtesy of
Erin Huntley

Pushing the Positive

The first sixteen weeks of a puppy's life are a critical period for your GSD. Her personality is beginning to take shape and patterns of behavior are forming. So, the time you put in now will pay off in spades later. Just as your training methods should always include positive reinforcement, your socialization approach should also be pushing the positive. If you're moaning about what a big job this will be and how much time it's going to take and you're not sure if your puppy really needs a focused socialization effort, remember this. The American Veterinary Society of Animal Behavior has a dire warning about what can happen if your GSD is inadequately socialized.

> ➢ "Behavioral issues, not infectious diseases, are the number one cause of death for dogs under three years of age."

Having a dog is all about dealing with possibilities and this is one of those times when you need to think about how your dog would get along if you were no longer in the picture. A socially adjusted canine, one that handles meeting new people well and enjoys exploring different places, increases her chances that she will continue to have a good life without you. Play the odds and maybe, just maybe, you can save your dog's life even if you aren't around.

Positive Preparations

I mentioned making the exploration of the world a positive experience and you can accomplish that in several different ways. Don't rush your puppy into situations. To a certain extent let her feel her way. You also need to remember that German Shepherds, even puppies, pick up on how you are feeling. If you're tense, they will tense up. So, try and relax and take your time. Putting your pup on a tight socialization schedule could do more harm than good. You want to take your pup out of her comfort zone, but gradually. If you're creating fear in your GSP you're going backward. Another way to push the positive is to be liberal with the treats when you're out and about. If Sheba loves little sweet potato nibbles make sure to have some of those in your pocket before your next get-to-know-the-world expedition takes place.

After you have had your GSP around the ranch for a week or two and she has had time to get used to the new faces and some of the routine that her life will have, it is time to start seriously socializing Sheba. You can expand her circle of acquaintances to extended family, friends, and neighbors. One of the best moves we ever made was getting our next-door neighbor introduced to Cody when the puppy first came home. Our neighbor is so comfortable now with our dog that he will look after Cody when we are away. It really is the best of both worlds for you and your GSD if some people close to you can help take care of the dog when needed. There is an intense bonding process happening during this early time. This is when your GSP learns to trust you and you start to have some faith in her.

Photo Courtesy of Colleen O'Connor

My Tip

> In order to solidify the bonding process during this socialization period, here are some no-no's. Never scare your pup "just for fun." Never tease your dog just "playing around." Last, but not least, never hit your GSP just "to teach them a lesson." GSDs need to know that you are a constant dependable, positive presence in their lives. You are their whole world, so don't make it a bad one.

You'll need to wait until your puppy's initial vaccination program is done and she has her immunity built up before expanding your horizons to total exposure, but don't wait to start the socialization process. Begin slowly but once the shots are over with, the sky is the limit. Now let's deal with some specific interactions that your puppy needs to have.

Dog Demeanor

It's crucial to allow your German Shepherd puppy to meet and associate with other dogs. You and Axel will get some socializing in puppy class but it's also important that puppies meet older dogs to continue their learning curve. Your GSP would have received some of the social basics in his first eight weeks of life from his mother and undoubtedly from his littermates. However, for Axel to become a full-fledged member of society he needs some adult modeling. Many people cringe at the suggestion of dog parks for their little baby but that's really where you'll find a cross-section of canine society.

Photo Courtesy of
Sherry Schuessler
schuesslerstudios.com

The Gang's All Here

- The Bullies who can't take no for an answer are always parked at the park.
- The Scaredy-Cats who cringe at all the barking are there.
- The Mighty Mouse little dogs who think they're ten feet tall strut their stuff there.
- The Cool Dudes who are only there for the sniffing, and maybe a drink of water, hang out here.
- The Laidback Hippie Hound with the bandana and a goofy smile on his face is sure to show up.
- The Big Boys who just stand around and don't do much of anything but drool are usually present.

With a mix of personalities like this, you'll need to be careful introducing little Axel to this rough and tumble environment. By the time you and your GSP put in an appearance at the local park you need to have at least some control over your puppy. Having a reliable degree of recall, coming when called, is a requirement because being on leash in the dog park is not a good idea. Being the only dog on a leash at the park is like a boxer having one hand tied behind his back. Axel needs to have mobility in order to move around and possibly get himself out of some tight spots.

Playing with the Big Dogs

"Monitor all interaction the first few weeks. If they get too aggressive in play, split them up and calm them down. When interacting with an adult dog do not let the adult dog dominate or "pin" the puppy. It can create a dog aggressive behavior in your new pup."

November Holley
Harrison K-9

Before taking your GSP to hang out with the big dogs, a little advance intelligence is in order. What's the best time to take a newbie to the dog park? Probably the quietest time possible, so in the beginning avoiding weekends, evenings, and first thing in the morning is the way to go. The dog park isn't a substitute for other exercise so make sure your pup has had a workout before the park jaunt. That will take the edge off his energy and make him a little more civilized once the gate to Fido Fields opens. OK, so here we go, you're at the dog park. Get out your mental checklist.

- Keep the visit short. No more than fifteen minutes, even less if you sense your GSP is overly anxious.

- Take the leash off. Tethered dogs can be extremely defensive and unleashed dogs can be aggressive in mixed company.

- I don't recommend toys or treats at the dog park. They're just an opportunity for a squabble.

- Pick up after your pet. Most parks provide plastic bags and garbage cans for disposal but bring your own bags just in case.

- Always keep track of your German Shepherd. Just because your dog is well-mannered doesn't mean everybody is and if trouble happens you want to cut it short before someone gets hurt.

From my experience, most older dogs will cut puppies some slack but if the youngster is too energetic or doesn't respect any boundaries, the big boys will put him in his place. That's all part of maturing and understanding the rules. You need to be sure that during your excursion nothing untoward happens, so keep your eyes peeled. Again, from my experience, most German Shepherds enjoy dog parks but don't necessarily want to play with other dogs. Cody has a good time but displays some aloofness and no other dog has really bothered him.

Pets and Pecking Order

Bringing a new German Shepherd puppy home and expecting him to get along with an existing, comfortable top dog and perhaps a temperamental kitty without thinking that scenario through is asking for trouble. Here's how to avoid complicating your life and maybe a large vet bill.

Senior Rover

Your older dog has had the house to himself. As far as he is concerned it is "his" territory, so when you bring your puppy into the equation it is a home invasion of sorts. You just need to do your best to make sure Rover welcomes the little invader with a wagging tail. If Rover is an older German Shepherd, they can be extremely protective of their territory, so you want to make sure that first introductions are brief and, most especially, non-threatening to both dogs. Initially that means some kind of neutral ground. The first encounter should be outside; it could be on the sidewalk down the street, the local park, anywhere that Rover doesn't claim as his own turf.

FUN FACT
Sniffing Out Friendships

German Shepherds have one of the most powerful senses of smell among dogs. They're frequently employed as sniffer dogs for police and aid in detecting drugs. A dog's sense of smell is believed to be at least 10,000 times as acute as ours. So, it's no wonder that dogs use their noses to interpret the world around them. From scent alone, dogs can distinguish between different people, sense anxiety or fear, and even determine the direction that an odor is coming from, due to the ability to move their nostrils separately. A dog's sense of smell is his primary method of communication with other dogs, and humans as well. By smell alone, your dog can determine another dog's sex, diet, and disposition.

- You'll need to have both dogs on loose leashes. Control is important but the dogs need to have a chance to sniff and move around.

- Smelling is all-important to dogs and each smell goes into their memory bank. You want Rover to recognize the puppy's smell for next time.

- Remember, dogs feel what you feel, so take some deep breaths and calm yourself down.

- If your German Shepherd puppy is overly excited, walk away and bring him back after a few minutes. You may want to try a short walk so the dogs get a chance to expend some energy. You'll be able to tell quite quickly how the newcomer is going over with the veteran.

The most important thing in this relationship-building exercise is to let the animals work out their own dynamic. The older dog will be dominant, and Rover should not be corrected if he has to put little Jaeger in his place. You may encounter a growl and maybe even a snap or two throughout and it is certainly something to keep your eye on but may just be a perfectly normal interaction between an established dog and a puppy who is unknowingly breaking the rules. If the first encounter went well, the next step would be having the two dogs spend some time in your front yard. Before moving into the house make sure that you take your GSP in first to let him get used to the interior sights and smells. Each time they meet, Rover and Jaeger can spend more time in each other's company, but you always need to have a keen eye out. German Shepherds and other dogs can be dependable but their behavior is never one hundred percent guaranteed.

Kitty Cats

Understanding prey drive is important when it comes to GSPs and cats. German Shepherds like to chase things. It's in their genes going back to Max von Stephanitz and the sheep-herding days. GSDs will have varying degrees of prey drive but it inevitably kicks into high gear when something small runs by. Like a cat. Young German Shepherd puppies don't have the tools to do much damage to Kitty but unless their behavior is modified early when it comes to the feline it could be a problem later. So, we need to teach the puppy that Kitty isn't prey and that you would dearly love for them to be friends and confidants. OK, maybe not confidants.

Before Zelda ever lays eyes on Kitty the best introduction for both of them should be a smelly one. It's really a sniff test. I would stress that it's important for the two animals to eventually meet each other in the environment that they will co-exist in, so for the purpose of this little exercise I'm assuming we have an indoor cat. Let your German Shepherd puppy get used to the cat's smell before a physical introduction. The first face-to-face could be with the pup in his crate and Kitty Cat free to explore in safety. It could be with both animals in the room with Zelda on a leash. Any movement toward the cat initially should be met with a firm "no" and this is a good time to work on reinforcing the "sit" command.

As you can imagine, keeping things under control is paramount. There is a theory that says cats can sense when puppies/dogs are under control and they will be more likely to engage if they feel it is safe to do so. If Kitty and Zelda can become friends, that's great but at least they should learn to tolerate each other. We'll go over some commands for Zelda in Chapter 12 but one of my most used commands with my five-year-old Shepherd, Cody, is "leave it." That one is very applicable to possibly saving Kitty's life and or your Shepherd's eyesight if push comes to claw. Depending on what kind of relationship you see developing, carefully monitored face-to-face encounters can take place with Kitty always having an obvious escape route. Cats are always a wild card so nothing is certain in the feline-canine relationship.

Pleased to Meet You

Dogs and kids just seem to go together, don't they? Properly socialized German Shepherds are generally very good with children but there is one thing to keep in mind about this particular breed. They have lots of energy (I mean that sincerely) and they act like puppies for a very long time. My five-year-old GSD has only now started to calm down a bit so in essence it's been a five-year puppyhood. I make that point because they can get overexcited and overstimulated quite easily, and unless they are watched closely in their interactions with kids, it can lead to problematic behavior.

My Tip
> Mixing toddlers and GSDs can be a particular challenge. From my experience, toddlers want to hang all over the dog and German Shepherds, not aware of their own size and strength, can easily knock the child down unintentionally. Special vigilance is required with little people and your German Shepherd puppy.

There are two classes of children as we all know. Your own well-behaved little darlings and everybody else's kids. Let's deal with GSD interaction and your family first.

Your Best Friend
Having a German Shepherd puppy grow up with your children can be a great experience for everyone involved. They have enough energy to match any child's stamina. They're incredibly smart and are easily trained for a variety of lifestyles. They're protective of their family and always want to please. They do demand a lot of attention so the more bodies on hand to help occupy that keen canine mind the better. But as with all situations, a few guidelines for the home side won't go amiss. The sooner they become house rules the better.

Don't torture the puppy. No hitting your new family member, no kicking, no pulling her tail.

Do pet her properly, from the head to the tail. German Shepherd puppies and adult dogs love the human touch, but in a respectful way.

Don't roughhouse. This means you! That's when kids and puppies get hurt.

Do play fetch. For a little while. Puppies need to burn off energy, plus it's an opportunity to practice commands like "drop" and "sit."

Don't disturb your GSP in her crate. That's her space and her refuge.

Do let sleeping dogs lie. Your puppy needs her rest and should not be disturbed during nap time.

Don't feed your German Shepherd human food. Even the smallest tidbit can end up being a mess on the living room carpet.

Photo Courtesy of Haley Belliveau

Do leave the puppy alone at meal times. Some dogs are finicky eaters as it is and don't need any distractions.

Don't take the puppy's toys away from her. Everyone loves her toys and so does Zelda, so let her have them.

Stranger Danger?

"If you're calm about something, the puppy will be too. If he startles and you baby him, he's going to think startling that is a good thing because it gets him attention. Don't coddle. There's nothing worse than a sharp shy adult Shepherd, and it's totally preventable."

Rebecca Dickson
GretchAnya German Shepherds

One of the characteristic traits of the German Shepherd is that they are typically suspicious of strangers. When a full-grown GSD lets out that deep, rumbling bark and the hair stands up on his back making the imposing animal look larger than he already is, it can be an incredibly intimidating sight. That behavior, believe it or not, is part of their DNA. Remember their background as shepherds, guarding the flock and fending off danger. While the sheep are out of the picture now, and danger is not so much a part of our lives, the genetic urge remains. "That's great," you say, "but how do I keep my German Shepherd puppy from getting into trouble when a stranger shows up?"

Well, the introduction of your German Shepherd puppy to a stranger is a two-way street. The puppy needs to know what behavior is expected of it but so does the stranger, adult or child.

Stranger Guidelines

1. Positive reinforcement. You want your German Shepherd to learn that guests are good and that a certain amount of fun accompanies a visit. Guests who dispense a treat or two may have the upper hand, and may in fact get to keep their hand. That's a little humor for those just tuning in.

2. Brief eye contact. Don't stare at the dog. It's rude to stare under any circumstances but prolonged eye contact with a German Shepherd you don't know can be interpreted as a challenge you don't want to make.

3. No sudden movements. If your guest gets nervous and starts to flail their arms around, that can be seen as an invitation to the dog to make a closer inspection.

4. No loud voices or shouting. Remember, a GSD senses emotions and moods and reacts accordingly. Gentle voices.

5. Let the dog come to you. I suggest making a fist and leaving your hand by your side for the dog to smell initially.

6. Even if the dog seems relatively friendly, don't pet them on the head. On the shoulders or along the back is more comfortable for the GSD.

7. If you can arrange it, no ringing doorbells or loud knocking. Those are things that seem to send most dogs into a frenzy.

Puppy Guidelines

1. Control the dog. If meeting the stranger outside, tell the German Shepherd when it is all right to approach the person. I always have a leash with me but only use it if absolutely necessary to maintain control. You can use the "sit and "stay" commands to give direction to the puppy.

2. If your guests are expected, make sure your puppy is well exercised so that when they do arrive Zelda will be less likely to have energy to burn, running circles around your guests and jumping up on them.

3. The treat/positive reinforcement approach works for you too. If your German Shepherd is treat-motivated you can reward her for listening to you and remaining under control. Don't forget the verbal praise. Some GSDs value that above all else.

4. Remember that you need to be calm so that is conveyed to your dog.

My Tip

> I have always found that making a dog feel confined when meeting strangers is problematic. If you can avoid putting your German Shepherd on a leash, avoid crating them or having them in a separate room from your guests, it is a better socialization situation for them. As always you know your dog best, so watch for signs of agitation or fear. If the dog isn't warming up to the situation then you do need to remove them from it.

This whole chapter has been focused on dealing with how to make your German Shepherd puppy a well-rounded social citizen. That means exposing them to as many things and experiences as possible so before we leave the social animal behind, I just wanted to give you a few more ideas on how to help your GSP move up the socialization ladder.

- An easy and non-threatening way of getting your puppy some exposure is to take her to an area where you can perhaps sit on a bench and watch the action. People will just naturally come over to you and want to talk about dogs; the children will want to pet the puppy.

- Exposing the dog to an assortment of noises is something to aim for. Walk by construction zones, skateboard parks, ballparks, hockey arenas, walking trails, airports.

- Dog parks but initially only from outside the fence where she can watch the action but not be intimidated by it.

- Go places where your German Shepherd puppy can see other animals, not just dogs but farm animals if possible, such as horses and cows.

- Car rides are excursions that will become part of your dog's daily life later on so getting her accustomed to piling into the family car and heading out as early as possible will be to everyone's benefit. Car sickness is an aspect of those jaunts that many GSD owners have to deal with. More on that in Chapter 15.

Coming up in the next chapter, we'll deal with the good and the bad of pack mentality. We'll also answer the question being asked in many households, "Why can't we all just get along?"

Photo Courtesy of
William Chilton

CHAPTER 9
Why Can't We All Just Get Along?

In this chapter we're going to deal with some of the possible relationships you might find yourself in when you bring a German Shepherd puppy, or two, home. First, though, we're going to deal with a couple of theories that each has its dogged supporters. Remember what I told you in my introduction. I'm not a dog trainer. I haven't conducted theoretical studies on wolf packs to examine hierarchy and determine how much wolf society can be seen in groups of dogs. So, if there is any controversy here, I don't own it. You're going to have to choose your own path in this one. What I will do is lay out a couple of schools of thought and then tell you what I've gathered in real life.

Photo Courtesy of
Anat Levi Hudaev
Photos by Hanna Sheleg

The Pack Mentality

Pack theory suggests that wolves live in a social hierarchy with the alpha animals (a male and a female) essentially in control of the others in the pack. This dominance theory goes on to suggest that dogs, likely having evolved from wolves, follow a similar order. Any unwanted behavior in the group, such as conflict resulting from aggression, is simply one animal trying to move up in rank, in essence trying to be the alpha animal. In this school of dog training then, any "aggressive" behavior, even a dog attempting to go through the doorway first, must be energetically corrected to show that humans are alpha and they always go first. Dogs wait. Some "dog" people have suggested that this theory of a pecking order is also transferable to your home, where the pack consists of you, your family of humans, and however many dogs may grace your doorstep. As far as the canines are concerned, the pack theory dictates that you need to establish yourself as the alpha and make sure that everything you do reinforces that social order. How you relate to your partner and children is another matter entirely.

Puncturing Pack Theory

On the flip side of this issue, some dog people believe that pack theory is a flawed concept, originating from research done on captive wolves who were living in an artificial environment. This school of positive reinforcement training believes that dogs respond best to training that rewards positive behavior, the stuff you want them to do, and ignores the negative behavior, the stuff you want them to forget. So, get out the treats, the attaboys, and the Frisbee.

The Real World

What I have found in the real world of dogs and behavior is this. Some training techniques work with some German Shepherds and some don't. "Why is that?" you ask. It's not rocket science really. Every dog has her own personality and can be an introvert or a boisterous baby who just wants to be a party animal. Some dogs only respond to a raised voice or a physical correction of some kind. By that I don't mean hitting the dog, but it might be something like this.

Cody and Coprophilia

When my German Shepherd, Cody, was a young puppy, he engaged in an activity that puzzles and disgusts many dog owners. He was fascinated by his own feces. So engrossed in it (I use that word intentionally), that he would eat his own poo. In those unenlightened days I would tell

Photo Courtesy of
Jenny Bowden

Photo Courtesy of George Haslam

him no, and perhaps hold his nose near a steaming pile and tell him no, over and over again. That didn't work.

One day we had a dog trainer visit the house and I explained how perplexed I was over Cody's fecal fascination. Mark, the trainer, explained that I should try this technique each and every time Cody performed his poo inspection. I was advised to stand very close to him and when he put his nose down to examine his excrement, I was to take three stiff fingers and jab him lightly in the side and say no. The theory was the jab would be a distraction for him, a reset in other words, and of course the "no" word would reinforce leaving his dung alone. Well, I spent far too much time standing very close to dog doo-doo but you know what? In the end Cody gave it up. Was he hurt in the process? Maybe his pride, when he wasn't allowed to continue his childish activity, but other than that he learned to walk away after doing his business.

The Real World: Part 2

STORY
Big Cats and Dogs

At the Oasis of the Siberian Tiger in Slovakia, an unlikely friendship was formed between three German Shepherd dogs and two of the Siberian Tigers living there. According to an article in the Daily Mail, the two tigers, Suria and Sunny, are deeply attached to the dogs, Blacky, Hugo, and Jenny. This unlikely friendship started because the animals were raised together and have been living alongside each other since they were just small kittens and puppies. As they have grown up their relationships have strengthened even further, and they have become a shining example that cats and dogs can get along well together.

Back in the real world I have found that portions of the pack theory work and relate to my daily life with an opinionated GSD and most of the positive reinforcement approach can be used on a regular basis. Each German Shepherd is a complex puzzle that only you will take the time to figure out. You may never figure it all out. That's OK too, as long as you make the lifelong attempt to keep at it. The tough thing about the human–German Shepherd relationship is that they figure you out long before you ever have handle on what makes them tick.

Having now dealt with some of the controversy in the dog training world, let's move on. I mentioned aggressive behavior early in this chapter. Everybody encounters it to one degree or another especially if there are other dog citizens in the house. Let's look at how to ease the animosity and keep things tranquil as possible on the domestic front.

Double Trouble?

It's tempting to think about bringing home two German Shepherd puppies from the same litter. Or even two unrelated GSPs. They'll have each other for company when you're not around. The kids will each have their own dog. We like dogs, we always wanted more than one. That's the rose-colored glasses look at adopting more than one puppy. Let's be more practical. Consider these things:

1. The cost. I'm not talking about the initial breeder and setup expenses. I'm referring to your time, the training they will require, and the fact that they should be socialized separately as much as possible.

It's for their mutual benefit, so they can become confident in their own right and not become dependent on each other.

2. Many dog trainers suggest that the puppies should be walked individually, sleep separately, eat separately, and only have a couple of pre-set play times with each other during the day. Is that feasible in your situation?

3. We are talking about German Shepherd puppies here. One puppy on its own requires an immense amount of dedication and commitment from the owners. I remember one late-night conversation with my wife where she was dead set on returning our GSP to the breeder because he was too much of a handful. We got over that bump in the road, but folks, one puppy is more than a handful.

If you've looked at these concerns and have no qualms about going ahead with bringing home two puppies, the more power to you, I say. Here are some more things to think about before you place your deposit on those siblings and say good-bye to any downtime.

- Make sure that the two pups don't spend so much time together that they develop a primary bond with each other. If they do, it can interfere with their training and broader socialization. They could just stop listening to you.

- Separation anxiety could be an issue despite your best efforts. Stay alert for early signs of this and it could mean the remedy is even less time together.

- If your and your partner's work schedules mean that you will both be away from the house for a good chunk of time, two GSPs doesn't add up. You won't be able to put in the required monitoring to keep Gunner and Gretchen out of trouble.

- Especially during the potty-training period, you won't be able to do it all yourself. Your partner and the kids will have to play a major role during this time.

- There is research that shows fighting and aggression between litter mates can be higher than with unrelated dogs. This can complicate socialization because the litter mate puts up with behavior that no stranger dog worth his kibble would.

Who Let the Dogs Out?

There's an ongoing fight in the house. One family member is continually getting into scraps with someone else in the family and they just won't give it a rest. It's like they are programmed to get on each other's nerves. But these aren't human kids, where everyone gets a timeout to calm down. They are doggy bros who can't see eye-to-eye, and if one of them is a German Shepherd, even a large puppy can cause a lot of damage in a free-for-all.

In the previous chapter we touched on how to introduce your new German Shepherd puppy to the existing dog in the household. But what if that doesn't seem to be working? What if they just can't seem to get along? When I was growing up my parents had a border collie and a boxer for a time. I can remember my mother trying to break up dog fights with a chair and a broom. The altercation was usually around meal time. Duke, the newcomer boxer, would inevitably finish his meal first and then head for the collie's dish. Lassie would have none of that and the snarling and snapping would break out. After a few tremendous tussles my mother realized that the two dogs just couldn't be fed at the same time in the same location. My mother didn't know it at the time but when she stopped feeding the dogs together, she was getting rid of one of the "stressors" in the canine relationship. So, let's dive a little deeper into the sibling rivalry situation.

Photo Courtesy of
Brent Ferguson

Changing Gears

You know that if the situation you have isn't working you need to change gears. The hardest part of modifying your domestic dog situation is determining what the specific irritants are. The second hardest part is figuring out how to change things up. Not all dogs will get along swimmingly but most can be trained to live together.

- Health check. Your GSP is probably reasonably healthy because you've been taking him to the vet periodically for shots and check-ups. It's a good idea to take the older dog in for a general checkup just to make sure there is no medical condition causing the aggression.

- Identify any stressors that could be leading to the dog fights. Those aggression triggers can be everything from food and toys to the doorbell ringing. Then remove or modify those triggers. For instance, our doorbell is in perfect working order but we have tape over it so no one uses it.

- If you truly believe your senior dog is being stressed by the German Shepherd, then you may need to call in a trainer who has expertise in positive behavior modification. It can be done but it takes some planning and time. Professional help can be a lifesaver.

- After consulting with a professional it may be that your two dogs cannot continue to live in the same house. If you must have an "only child," spend some time finding the right family to take your other pet into their lives. It's a tough decision but the safety of your dogs is paramount, which means you have to do the right thing.

Another important thing to remember is that the resident dog's aggression toward your German Shepherd may not just be based on one thing. Just as when humans lose their temper, for dogs it often is not what just happened but a number of things leading up to the growling and the snapping that has tipped the dog over the bite threshold. Slowly removing possible aggression triggers one by one can get things back on an even keel.

My Tip
➢ Increase the amount of exercise for both dogs. This may help take the edge off their behaviors. Tired puppies will be less inclined to antagonize each other.

That tip is the perfect segue into the next chapter. You don't want a dog who is a couch potato hanging around the house. Some studies put the percentage of obese dogs in the U.S. at more than fifty percent. If you start your dog's lifestyle off on the right four feet you shouldn't have to worry about him becoming one of those heavyweight statistics.

CHAPTER 10
Exercising Your Options

Photo Courtesy of Jamie St. Martin

German Shepherds have been bred to have energy. Lots of it. There is an old joke among GSD owners. The good news is you are the proud owner of a GSD. The bad news is you have to exercise him. Well, it's not really bad news but you're going to find that it's definitely more of a marathon than a sprint. The best way to deal with the insatiable workout demands of your dog is to have a schedule, be faithful to that timetable, and always make sure Thor is tired at the end of the day. Your approach to exercising a German Shepherd puppy will be completely different than dealing with an adult dog so I'll break things up into two sections. But before we go there, I want to mention something about living in the German Shepherd world. Once you have a GSD and start talking to trainers, and start going onto German Shepherd forums on social media, you'll find that there are at least two opinions on how to approach everything in GSD World. That also applies to exercising your puppy. There is one school of puppy performance that is extremely conservative, advocating some exercise but nothing extremely structured, letting the puppy expend his energy running around and perhaps playing with some of his puppy peers. The other school of thought says that German Shepherds are bundles of energy, especially puppies, and we should help them expend that energy in order to keep them somewhat civilized. My experience with my own GSD and observing others lands me somewhere in the middle of both camps. Call me a master of moderation.

Baby Steps

"Young puppies should not be over exercised, 10-15 minutes at the most, walking at first no further than 2 houses or a city block and back. Jogging with a young dog of 12 months or younger is not good for their hips. Puppies are developing their bones until they are 12-13 months of age."

Sharon
Pretorian Kennel

Your puppy is growing fast. Everything little Thor has is developing at a rapid rate. And that can be a problem. Too much exercise, and the wrong kinds of activity can damage your German Shepherd puppy for life. The reason? Blame it on something called "growth plates." These are located on the ends of your little dog's long leg bones and they consist of cartilage that gradually hardens into bone as Thor grows. Overly strenuous exercise, jarring activities like jumping or running down stairs, can damage the growth plates and leave a German Shepherd puppy with deformities like bowed legs or even early development of dysplasia. So, until the plates close and are finished growing (which happens around eighteen months old) only moderate exercise is recommended. I would

suggest that no forced exercise be included in your puppy program. Here's my take on things.

Don't encourage jumping or leaping games. Definitely no leaping in the air for Frisbees. By this I mean not over and over again. Once in a while is fine. Remember, I said moderation.

Do go on lots of walks. Puppies can stop and sniff at their own pace. You might even lose a few pounds.

Don't try and turn your puppy into a Stairmaster. Some stair climbing in the course of a day is all right but not as an exercise program.

Do play lots of fetch or whatever version of fetch your puppy can manage. GSPs are ball crazy so you'll have no trouble engaging them. Getting them to bring the ball back to you and drop it is a whole other issue.

Don't put a leash on your puppy and take them jogging or cycling. You need to give your dog the opportunity to take natural breaks and rest. Especially stay off hard surfaces such as concrete when exercising your German Shepherd puppy. Turf is king.

Photo Courtesy of Eve Dering

Do play games like hide and seek. Some running, some sniffing, some mental concentration, it doesn't get any better than that. After a few minutes of this I can see puppy's eyes closing and game time turns into nap time.

Don't overdo the total amount of exercise. A general guideline that some GSD dog trainers recommend is five minutes of exercise per month of age. So, a four-month-old is good for twenty minutes at a time with you being the judge of how many times a day you exercise Thor.

Do see if they like the water. The earlier a puppy learns to swim the more exercise time can be devoted to the water. As with humans, it's a very body-friendly exercise for your best friend.

A last word on puppies and exercise. They are enthusiastic partici-pants in every game, every walk, every stick-throwing venture. Most of them don't know when to stop and they will run until they drop if you al-low it. Don't do that. It's usually when a puppy has exceeded his limits that he gets into trouble, physically and socially. You should become a master of moderation too.

Photo Courtesy of Brian Nainby

Mature Mambo

When your German Shepherd hits the heady days of adulthood, sometime around the eighteen-month mark, Thor's exercise options and indeed his physical requirements change significantly. He will still be a ball of fire but you are able to structure his exercise time so that in coincides with your exercise time. That can be a real time-saving bonus when you don't have to schedule for two different workout periods. Before we run too far down that road, I think it's important to mention a guideline that I religiously adhere to.

My Tip

➢ Don't exercise your GSD after eating. They may want to but the dog needs time to digest. Large breeds like German Shepherds are susceptible to something called bloat. That happens when the animal's stomach twists and if immediate veterinarian help is not obtained it can be fatal. Make sure everyone relaxes after the meal.

Now that you have an adult GSD you can start testing her limits and making sure that when every day comes to an end you have a tired dog on your hands.

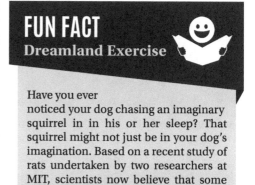

FUN FACT

Dreamland Exercise

Have you ever noticed your dog chasing an imaginary squirrel in in his or her sleep? That squirrel might not just be in your dog's imagination. Based on a recent study of rats undertaken by two researchers at MIT, scientists now believe that some animals may dream about actual events from their daily lives. So next time you see your dog having a dream, he might just be reliving the highlights of his day!

- Dog Paddling. GSDs love the water and if you taught Mischa the basics early on, she will love to swim out and fetch things back to shore. Swimming is the best exercise for German Shepherds of all ages.

- Trail Mix. Hiking with your dog is good exercise for both of you but it will be more mentally and physically stimulating for Mischa than a turn around the neighborhood park.

- Packing on the Pounds. To help tire your GSD out you can outfit her with a backpack with some lightweight items to begin. If you're camping and your dog is in good condition, they can help carry the load.

- Jog On. You have every reason to take your GSD with you when you resume your jogging routine. When you're not on the run, Mischa would also make a good cycling partner.

*Photo Courtesy of
Sherry Schuessler
schuesslerstudios.com*

- Frisbee Fanatic. You can get a lot of mileage out of a Frisbee. The soaring, floating disc gives a German Shepherd endless hours of conditioning and entertainment.

- Childish Games. Don't forget the puppy pastimes. Hide and seek, ball toss especially with a ball launcher.

- In Your Face. Tug-of-war is a friendly test of strength that occupies some time. Useful indoors on a rainy day.

- Figuring It Out. Food puzzle toys can double as a meal and great mental stimulation as well. Couldn't we all use more of that?

That last point about mental stimulation leads me to the more thoughtful part of this chapter. Your German Shepherd can be made as fatigued by mental stimulation as any hike on a mountain trail. If you can get to an off-leash area, and you have good recall, just let your GSD wander and sniff. Her senses will be so preoccupied that you won't even realize how tired Mischa is until she falls asleep before dinner. Coming up with ideas to challenge your GSD is where your own creativity can really shine.

We have a large plastic barrel in our backyard. I alternately put Cody's Frisbee on top of the upside-down barrel, in the upright container, and under the overturned barrel. I make Cody sit about fifty yards away each time, then release him to run to the barrel and retrieve his toy, sometimes by standing on his hind legs to put the bite on the Frisbee on the top or sometimes having to push the barrel over to get the Frisbee. He is content to go lie down for a few minutes after a ten-minute workout of barrel Frisbee.

Now much of your German Shepherd's mental stimulation is going to come from the training that you and your dog spend time on. Coincidentally, that's where we're going in the next chapter that I like to call "Who's Training Who?"

CHAPTER 11
Who's Training Who?

"Don't lose your temper when training. If they are not catching on it's because the owner is doing something wrong in the foundation of the training and has skipped steps"

Tracy Berg
vom Haus Berg German Shepherds

Photo Courtesy of Mark Hager

The most important component of your German Shepherd's training program is you. That's because your GSD is a natural; Brunhilde is going to pick up what she needs to know relatively quickly. In fact, if you don't pay attention, your dog will gradually take over the agenda. The weak link in the training department is usually the human being. Most often, that is because the approach is unfocused, a little bit of this, combined with some of that, do it once in a while, and the job is done. Well, not so fast. To stay on track, here are some questions you need to ask yourself before ever picking up a leash or putting treats in your pocket.

- What do you want to achieve in your training sessions?
- What are your expectations?
- What are your specific goals?
- How much time are you able to commit?

Even if your ultimate goal is to have a well-behaved family pet, the overall approach to training your GSD will not be much different than someone who is looking to go into competitive sports like Schutzhund, which focuses on tracking, obedience, and protection work. The starting point, the underlying basics, are the same. If you have clearly outlined your goals and mapped things out, you and Brunhilde will get there. German Shepherds want to work. The desire to be occupied is in their DNA. Your job is to make training one of the activities your dog loves to do.

Principles for Progress

✔ Consistency. GSDs are extremely bright and they learn new behaviors enthusiastically. That's the easy part of this principle. The harder piece is reinforcing through repetition what has been learned until that behavior is second nature. It needs to become a habit.

Photo Courtesy of Cindy Harr

✔ Timing is critical. If you can reinforce or correct an action immediately, as it's happening, German Shepherds will learn the lesson right then and there. Being on top of things, being observant, will speed up the pace of your training immeasurably.

✔ KISS Method. Keep It Succinct and Simple. German Shepherds don't speak English so throwing a whole bunch of words around isn't going to help them. Only use words that mean something, that represent the command itself.

✔ Short & Successful. Your sessions should be brief, ten minutes at a time, and always ending on a positive high note.

✔ Patience & Praise. Combine these two and you are definitely barking up the right tree. If a dog senses anger, they focus on that, so staying patient is key. Praise is a reward; coupling the verbal positive with petting and the occasional treat takes reinforcement to a higher level.

✔ Take a Pass on Punishment. There is no room for punishing your German Shepherd at all but especially during training. If your dog isn't giving you the desired behavior, then step back and look for the weak link. You shouldn't have to look too far.

✔ Be a Leader. Take charge and show your GSD what you want her to do. Some trainers use the terms "alpha" or "master" to indicate the owner's role. Call yourself whatever you want, but be a leader.

Different Strokes

Many people train their dogs solely with verbal commands and that can obviously achieve the desired effect. There are other methods, perhaps in addition to verbal training, that you might want to incorporate into your regimen. Some trainers like to use hand signals when working with their GSDs. Here's why it might make sense for you to add manual motions to your training repertoire.

Body Language Benefits

Photo Courtesy of
Jordyn Gilbert

• Hand signals are subtle when you want to communicate with your German Shepherd quietly. They are also useful for giving direction at a distance.

• Gestures can maintain communication between owners and hearing-impaired dogs. Older dogs with failing hearing will have one less excuse for ignoring you.

• Many canine competition sports use hand signals so you would be ahead of the game by getting started early with a hands-on approach.

• Hand signals can reinforce the bond between owner and dog. They force the dog to have eyes on their human constantly, which is what every trainer aims for.

• Using verbal commands and hand signals together can accelerate your GSD's learning. That's because dogs are geared naturally to watch for physical signals from their human.

If you haven't ever thought about using hand signals, try experimenting with your own dog. I quite often take my GSD, Cody, on off-leash walks because of the rural property we live on. Sometimes when we are on trails, when we come to a fork, he will look at me before proceeding. If I gesture right or left, off Cody goes down that trail. Watching you and your hands is a natural thing for German Shepherds, so incorporating some hand signals in your daily routine might just give everybody a little more direction.

Clicker Training

The use of a clicker falls squarely into the positive reinforcement strategy that I've advocated throughout this book. Before we go into how the clicker system works, I just want to return to a brief discussion of the German Shepherd breed.

What I've found with my own GSD and with some others I've known is that they are a very sensitive animal. People who aren't familiar with GSDs might say, "Sensitive? How can that big bruiser with the intimidating bark be sensitive? He looks like he wants to tear my leg off." Most of the time that impression is just a stereotype picked up unconsciously. Shepherds take what you say to them, and what you do to them, to heart. So, if you shout at them frequently or are inclined to push them around, over time they will begin to react badly to that negative discipline. I'm not above telling Cody to go lie down and take a timeout because he has decided to have a dig by his favorite shrub. I would never take him and put him in his crate and keep him there as punishment for digging. As you go through your days of training remember that your GSD is a dog, but he is also one of your best friends. Treat him how you would want to be treated.

My Tip

> *In dog training, jerk is a noun, not a verb.*

- Dr. Dennis Fetko

Back to the positive things about clicker training. It's a simple technique. It doesn't take a brain surgeon to master it. From my perspective it's most beneficial when initially training your dogs. You might want to leave it behind eventually in favor of voice commands and hand signals but that's a choice you can make later on. Here's a quick overview of how a clicker can make you a master dog trainer. OK, that's a bit of an exaggeration but the system does work and no animals are harmed during the process.

Click Bait

With clicker training you are conditioning your German Shepherd to perform tasks with the understanding that when she sits, for instance, the clicker will sound and she will get a treat. The key is to make sure the reward is dispensed concurrently with the clicker sound, so for the dog, the sound and the treat have an intimate connection. If you want to delve more deeply into the psychology of how and why this approach works check into these methods of learning:

- Classical Conditioning. Learning by association as in Pavlov's salivating dog experiment

- Operant Conditioning. Learning through a system of rewards and punishments

The Personal Touch

There may come a time in your training when you hit a wall. It might be something simple, like getting Brunhilde to walk properly on a leash. Why do I bring up that particular example? It's simple. That's an area where I've always struggled with my dog. When I found that I wasn't making any progress with leash walking I decided to go to a personal dog trainer. It can be an expensive option but it's also effective. Rather than frustrate yourself and your German Shepherd, it might be worth your while to go to someone with fresh ideas. If the problem you're experiencing is related to your dog's behavior, such as chewing or barking, it's important to make a move sooner rather than later because you want to deal

FUN FACT
Buddy the Dog

German Shepherds are frequently used as service dogs, but did you know that the first Seeing Eye Dog was a German Shepherd? Her name was Buddy, and she and her owner, Morris Frank, led the way for future service dogs who now assist people with a variety of disabilities. In 1928, Buddy came to America from Switzerland, where she had been trained by American dog breeder Dorothy Harrison Eustis. On June 11, 1928, Morris Frank and his dog made a historic trip across New York City's very busy West Street, shattering the disbelief of onlookers who had never seen a dog lead the blind. Buddy served her owner until her death in 1938. "Buddy delivered to me the divine gift of freedom," said Frank.

with any behavioral problems while your dog is relatively young, say in the first twelve months of her life.

You'll also need to make sure that the training you select is in line with your own personal philosophy. Most reputable trainers will spend some introductory time with you to make sure you're on the same wavelength. One important question to ask: "Have you trained German Shepherds before?" I have seen trainers who have no idea how to work with a GSD. Those people will only add to your problems. Here's a quick reminder of some general approaches that are available.

Training Techniques to Think Through

1. Positive reinforcement. I put this in the number one spot because it's the technique that mostly works for me. Good behavior is rewarded; non-compliant behavior receives no reward or acknowledgment.

2. Alpha/Pack. In this approach you're the alpha in your relationship with your German Shepherd and everything you do supports your dominance. You might find you want to mix some of the techniques to achieve what works for you individually. Alpha and positive reinforcement can work together up to a point.

Photo Courtesy of
Colleen Toia

Photo Courtesy of
Emily Birish

3. Electronic method. This involves the use of collars that deliver a shock when the dog is showing unwanted behavior. It's a punishment method and I would suggest it only as a last resort, used in consultation with a professional trainer familiar with the devices and the possible repercussions.

If you find that you work well in groups with your German Shepherd, advanced obedience classes could also be a solution when you become stuck in your own training. If you are extremely goal oriented, you might consider preparing Brunhilde for one of the various Canine Good Neighbor tests. There is a good one offered by the American Kennel Club. This type of instruction can provide a good basis for advanced training that many German Shepherds participate in.

Now that we've covered some of the basic types of training, it's time to deal with some of the fundamental commands that every German Shepherd needs to know. It would be easier if the dogs came with a command package already installed but we haven't advanced that far in the dog training world. You'll have to be your own mechanic on this one.

CHAPTER 12
Command Performance

"German Shepherds are both easy and hard to train. They are smart and learn quickly, but they will also find the loopholes in your training and exploit them. Consistency is extremely important; you need to be as black and white as possible and set firm boundaries. No means no, not 'sometimes'."

Celeste Schmidt
Dakonic German Shepherds

FUN FACT
Intelligent Pups

In Stanley Coren's book The Intelligence of Dogs, German Shepherds were ranked third for intelligence, behind border collies and poodles. This high level of intelligence makes German Shepherds ideal search and rescue, service, therapy, and police dogs. German Shepherds can do almost anything and are so smart that you may wonder if your dog is understanding everything you say!

I take something I call my "patience pill" every morning. It's not really a "chill pill." It's more of an adjustment to my mindset, usually done while contemplating a bowl of porridge. I know that when I go out with my German Shepherd, Cody, to practice commands, good as he is, I still need to take a breath and remember to keep my composure and be tolerant. You see, dogs want to please and they will try hard, but they don't always get it right the first time they try something, or the second time or the third.

So, when you and your pup start out working on her basic set of commands, it needs to be done with self-control and some restraint on your part. And treats, did I mention treats?

You can start working with your German Shepherd puppy as soon as you bring her home, which should be no sooner than the eight-week mark. When they are that young, one of the first things they need to learn is their handle, their alias, their nom de dog. Just because it says Bella on her name tag doesn't mean she knows she is Bella. As we work through this chapter we will use the name "Bella" in reference to your new puppy, whatever their name may be.

Name Recognition

One of the first things that you need to make sure of is that Bella will always look at you when asked. All her life. The simplest way of teaching that (as with all commands) is the two-pronged approach. Say your dog's name, and when she looks up at your hopeful face, clap your hands, say yes or whatever physical/verbal encouragement you want to give, and then deliver a treat from your full pocket. The name exercise can be incorporated into any other routine that you are working on but as with all exercises, don't overdo it. If Bella doesn't look at you when her name is called, try this to jog her memory.

1. Attach her leash.

2. Call her name.

3. If she doesn't respond, call her name again and give the leash a little tug, which will almost certainly cause Bella to look at you.

4. Deliver verbal praise, closely followed by the most important thing in your German Shepherd's eyes, the treat.

I know you love your dog. Bella-Wella is one of the most precious things in your life, but at least when your German Shepherd is young you need to refrain from using cute names or nicknames for Bella. She needs to get used to her given name first before all the love handles that will come her way throughout a dog's life. I suggest that you choose a name with no more than two syllables so that it is easy to say and/or shout at the dog park. Bartholomew does not exactly roll off the tongue with ease.

Sit

"Luring" is a term used in the dog training world to describe how to employ the promise of a treat to prompt the desired action. Luring is never more useful than when it's time to teach your dog to plant her posterior. When teaching your GSP how to sit, take the treat and hold it right in front of her nose. Slowly raise the treat a little bit at a time so that the dog raises her head. Most puppies will automatically assume the sitting position as they enthusiastically follow the treat and try to get a nibble. Once they're sitting, deliver the "sit" command and of course hand over the treat. Repeat until you have to go and sit down. Now would also be the time to think about introducing hand signals to coincide with your verbal commands, if you can handle all that pressure at once.

Come

"Come" is probably the most important command you will ever teach your dog. It could save her life in some circumstances. So, you need to get your puppy to respond to the recall command early and practice often. Here's the technique that has worked for me. You are out with Bella in the backyard. It's best to be in a contained space where no one can escape and the distractions will hopefully be at a minimum. Walk backward facing your GSP with a treat in your hand calling her name and "come." Odds are Bella will run toward you. Deliver the treat with much praise and do it several more times but again not excessively. You may have to

conduct several sessions like this on different days before Bella starts associating the move toward you with the "come" command. At a time of your choosing stop using Bella's name and just use the command.

My Tip

> Practice collar grabs at the same time as you are working on recall. This will get your dog used to you holding her collar. In an emergency you need to be able to "collar" your German Shepherd easily to keep her from harm or at least away from the birthday cake.

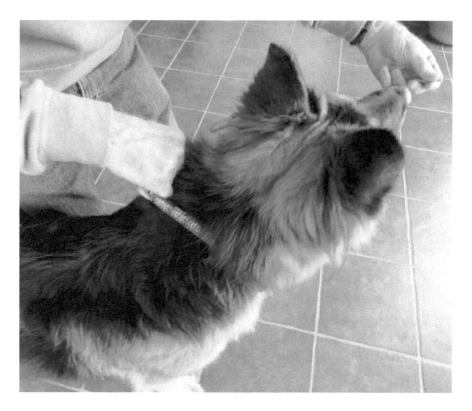

Do Not Do This!

Never recall your dog to you and then punish her in any way. If you do you are teaching Bella that there may be unpleasant repercussions for her if she comes so she could be hesitant to come or not listen to the command at all. This is where your patience may be tested but take a chill pill and a deep breath.

Leave It

I take a closed fist approach to teaching a German Shepherd how to keep her mouth off things. Now remember how hard this is for a dog to do. Their first inclination when they see something they want to investigate further, is to go have a sniff and then clamp their pearly whites on whatever it is. Some of the things they may want to taste could kill them. So, you need to have a command that tells your dog to refrain from her natural behavior. It's a tough ask and it may take a while and a lot of dog slobber on your hands but it's a must have in your command arsenal.

1. Place delectable, irresistible treat in open hand in a location where Bella can easily wander over to investigate.

2. When Bella makes a grab for said treat, close fist and say "No, leave it." She may slobber and nibble your fingers but be strong and just sit there with closed fist.

3. When Bella stops her oral assault, open fist and repeat procedure.

4. After innumerable attempts by your puppy to maul your hand she will get the idea that she cannot have the treat so at some point she will just sit there when you have your hand open and tasty treat exposed. I remember watching the drool cascade off Cody's chin when we were at this stage.

5. Once you've ascertained that your German Shepherd is sitting there, more or less under control, you can then say "OK" and let her have the treat.

6. Repeat until your dog just looks at you with those big brown eyes as if to say, "I get it. Enough already."

Stay

You've still got those treats handy, right? OK, let's continue. There are some dog trainers that say you don't need a "stay" command. They believe that when you give your dog a direction, such as "sit," for example, that the dog should just sit forever until you release them. That may be fine for some folks but it never seemed to work out that way for me. I've always used a three-part process to implement and release a stay command.

1. First, I use a "sit" or "down" command.

2. Then the "stay" direction.

3. Lastly to end the stay, my release command is always "break."

"But wait a second," you say. "You haven't told me how to do a stay." And you're right, I was getting a little ahead of myself. Let's back up and try that again, stay with me now. How about this?

1. Put your dog in the sit position.

2. Place your extended arm in front of you with the palm of your hand facing Bella.

3. Say "stay" and take a step or two back. After your German Shepherd has remained in the sit position for a few seconds use whatever word you want to release Bella and give her a treat.

4. If your dog breaks her sit right away, restart the sit with arm outstretched and issue the "stay" command with no steps. Proximity is important sometimes and if a dog feels you are within reach of them, they are more reluctant to move without permission.

You will ultimately want to work on putting some distance between your dog and yourself while she is in "stay" mode, but that should only be done when Bella is reliable within an arm's length or two.

Lie Down

Here's a question for you. Do you cross your legs when you sit down regardless of what your doctor says? Why do you think you do it? I can tell you why I cross my legs when seated. It makes me more comfortable. Calms me down in a way, so that if I'm at a boring party and I have to listen to someone talk about themselves, I can sip my wine, grin, and bear it. Now your German Shepherd won't find herself at too many parties, I'm imagining, but they sure do like to relax when they think things are under control around them. One of the ways dogs like to kick back and relax is by lying down, so it's a natural thing for them to do. Your job is to make it natural for them to listen to you and lie down on command.

1. Have Bella sit. Show her that you have her most favorite, wonderful treat in your hand.

2. Take your hand with the treat in it, put it in front of Bella's nose, and then move your hand ahead of her and down. The puppy's natural inclination will be to follow her nose right to the ground. Don't forget to say "lie down" when she accomplishes this.

3. Presto, you have a downward dog. Deliver treat and profuse praise.

4. After it has been mastered from the sitting position, practice the "lie down" command from a standing start.

Drop It

The theory behind this particular exercise is to get your German Shepherd involved in a trading game. My GSD is a ball hound. Most of them are. For the longest time as a puppy, Cody would run around with a ball in his mouth and not even think about dropping it or giving it up to any human. The ball was one of his prized possessions. Until one day he realized that I could throw his ball, and he could chase it. He loved chasing the ball but still didn't want to give it up once he had it. I'm sure it was a conundrum for him. A ball in the mouth versus using his prey drive and chasing down the orange ball. He never would have worked it out on his own and that's where I stepped in. I figured that if Cody loved that one ball so much, he might love two balls twice as much.

1.   I went out into the yard with two orange balls and a very enthusiastic puppy. With his focus squarely on me I would throw one of the balls a short distance away.

2.   Cody would energetically sprint after the ball, grab it in his mouth, and then his natural inclination was to prance over to me, not to drop the ball, but just to taunt me that he had the ball and I didn't.

3.   I would then show Cody the second ball in my possession, point to his ball and then the ground, and say "drop." This of course didn't work for the first few times, so then I introduced the treat element.

4. Armed with some small pieces of freshly cooked chicken I said to Cody "drop it" and waved a piece of chicken under his puppy nose.

5. Cody dropped the ball, ate the treat, and then looked at me standing there with a ball in each hand.

6. Here's how the process played out after that. Many

more ball throws, more treats, until finally Cody would come back with his ball and drop it on command.

7. Eventually treats were taken out of the equation, replaced by the two balls.

8. The "drop" command eventually became transferable to sticks, stones, and small dead animals.

By the way, I still use two balls at a time when playing fetch with Cody because we can get twice as much exercise done in half the time if we really concentrate on the game. So just to summarize the fundamentals of the "drop" exercise:

- Give Bella one of her favorite toys.

- Use treats to convince Bella to give up the toy.

- Each time she releases, use

"drop" command, give her a treat and verbal praise.

- If your dog isn't treat-oriented (it happens) use a low value toy to begin with and work up the treasured scale of toys.

- Eventually treats can be removed from equation to be replaced by "yes" and "good girl."

Off/Down

This command can be used to keep Bella off your favorite chair or the sofa. It can be used to cut short a counter-surfing episode. It even helps stop your dog from jumping up on you when you come home at the end of the day. It's a really versatile command but teaching it can be problematic. It's not a behavior you want to encourage so you have to wait until you catch the scoundrel in the act. And like any of the exercises you teach your four-legged fur child, consistency is paramount.

If Your Dog Jumps Up on You

You need to break your German Shepherd of this bad habit as soon as possible. If your dog jumps up on someone when she is full-grown, she can knock them down and cause injury, especially to elderly people. So, it all starts with you and here are a couple of tactics to use.

Off Options

- When your GSP jumps up on you, turn your back on her and say "off!" A stern tone of voice is required for the command word. Remember, your dog just wants you to engage with her and turning your back shows you are not going to pay any attention to her if she behaves this way. She will get it eventually.

- If you see your dog coming, and you know she is excited and about to jump up on your clean shirt that you've just taken out of the dryer, put your knee up so that Bella cannot plant her paws on your chest. Timing and balance are crucial.

- The last option you can employ is anticipating your German Shepherd as she makes her move to jump up on you. Grab her forepaws as she is standing on her hind legs and walk her backward. She will most likely sit at this point and as she does you need to issue the "off" command. You need to be careful not to turn this one into something that Bella considers a game.

The comforting thing to know about jumping up is that it is one behavior, coupled with the dog's age and your dogged persistence, that Bella will outgrow.

Surfin' Safari

Now what can you do with a German Shepherd that likes to surf? Inside your house. Roasts swiped off the counter, cake stolen from the kitchen table, conspicuous clumps of dog hair left on the sofa. Let's start with the sofa.

You know when in training mode with your dog you always need to have treats in your pockets. So, when you see Bella stretched out on the sofa you need to take a couple of those delectable delights, place them on the rug or floor, and say "off" while pointing to the treats. Bella will abandon her comfortable perch for the food. Again, repetition is the only cure for this disease. Even if you're tired and you just got home from work and the last thing you want to do is correct your dog's behavior. Dogs understand consistency.

Sometimes dogs are just overpowered by smells. You can tell they aren't actually thinking about what they're doing. Instinct has taken over. That's the case when food is out on a counter or a table. This is when having a large dog like a German Shepherd can actually be a disadvantage. They can stand on their hind legs and make a clean sweep of whatever might be out in the open. Here are some things you can do to make sure Bella minds her manners.

1. Keep the countertops and tabletops clear of food when you're not immediately using them. This means everyone in the household including the teenager who makes a sandwich and leaves all the makings sitting out on the counter. If there is no temptation, there is no crime.

2. If there is a big meal underway, say Thanksgiving dinner, and there is food absolutely everywhere, remove your dog from the area. If they have a day bed somewhere or a rug that you habitually locate them to, tell them to go to their bed. Keep them in place and out of the way until the gourmet extravaganza is under control.

3. If your German Shepherd habitually hangs out where food preparation and delivery are underway, make sure that some little treats go into her food bowl or onto the floor in an out of the way spot. If Bella realizes that she is going to receive some good stuff if she stays down, then that is likely to become an ingrained habit.

Loving the Leash

I've saved the best for last. Walking on a leash isn't so much of a command as it is a way of life. I have seen dogs that learned to walk on leash without pulling very quickly and I have seen the personal dogs of trainers who were bad citizens when on a leash. Once again there are no secrets to success here.

Consistency. Always do the same things when leash training so your dog knows what to expect and what is expected.

Practice. Use the leash. Sometimes when your dog doesn't seem to be catching on as quickly as you would like, you are tempted to avoid situations where you have to put them on a leash. Instead of a walk they go into the back yard. Or to the dog park where you can get them off leash ASAP. Don't do that.

Rewards. Give your German Shepherds rewards for good leash behavior. If it's treats and food, great. If not, make play time a little longer. If your smart girl realizes good things come with leash time Bella will be good. After all, it's in her best interest.

Patience. Need I say more?

Start 'Em Young

The best thing you can do when that eight-week-old comes home is get the collar and leash out and put them on. Under supervision, of course. Let little Bella wear her collar and drag the attached leash around during the day so that it becomes part of her scenery. You can even go for leash walks around the house. Go bother someone who is doing her

homework. Interrupt the video game marathon. See what's cooking in the kitchen. You'll need to wait until your GSP is a bit older to formally start leash training. Three months of age is typically when German Shepherds can begin to make sense of training so when you're ready, try this.

- Get yourself a fanny pack. Fill it with treats. It's a handy tool to have when your hands will be full with the leash and dispensing treats.

- Decide what side your dog will walk on. I find the left side is more natural for me and it is the "traditional" side, FYI.

- Start walking briskly with a loose leash in your right hand, and your left hand, with treats, by your side.

- Your puppy should naturally gravitate to that left side. Keep walking and dispense the occasional treat as long as Bella stays by your side. After several expeditions you can try leash walking with fewer treats.

- If your dog pulls, change your direction immediately and walk the other way. The idea is to plant the concept in your dog's brain that she has to follow you, not the other way around.

- Whenever Bella follows you, make sure the treats flow.

- Some dogs are quick learners, some are resistant learners. You'll soon know which you have on your hands.

So that's a quick overview of some of the foundational work that you should be doing with your growing German Shepherd. Yes, it's a bit of work but it pays off in the long run with a very civilized canine member of your family. If your appetite has been whetted for more training and you want to learn where else there is to go with your German Shepherd's education, well, the next chapter I call "Dogs with Jobs" is designed just for you.

CHAPTER 13
Dogs with Jobs

"The German Shepherd Dog is one of the most intelligent and active breeds, used worldwide for many different jobs: Guard dog, seeing eye dog, therapy dog, service dog, military dog, police dog, drug sniffing dog, rescue dog and a lot more."

Klaus Langenbach
Vom Geisterholz Kennel

S ometimes you just know that your dog needs more to do. There are signs. It could be the fact that Boris is standing there just vibrating with excess energy. You've done obedience training until it's coming out your ears with the four-footed super-athlete and fed him his lunch but it's not enough. Boris is cut out for bigger things. He wants to be an actor on a grander scale. He suspects there must be more to life than the backyard, the local park, and rides to The Home Depot. Boris has that look in his eye like he's going to start running around looking for trouble. Well, maybe he should be actually looking for trouble. I mean really. Maybe he needs a job.

Photo Courtesy of
Katy Howard

SAR Dogs

Search and rescue dogs make a point of looking for trouble. But their job is to help in those situations. Many civilian-run SAR organizations suggest that you begin training your puppy as young as twelve weeks for a service role. German Shepherds are one of the most highly prized breeds for this work. It can be a lengthy and expensive preparation process though; it's not uncommon to take several years and owners can spend thousands of dollars getting ready to take the qualifying exams. In general, SAR dogs fall into two categories.

1. Air-scenting dogs. These tracking machines work off-lead and follow any airborne human scent.

2. Trailing dogs. They work with a leash and follow a ground track.

You need to be extremely committed to get involved with search and rescue. SAR dogs must have extremely high prey drive. There is no paycheck but there is definitely payback.

Schutzhund

The German word schutzhund means "protection dog." It's a sport designed specifically for the German Shepherd. You'll remember good old Max von Stephanitz from Chapter One. Von Stephanitz was involved in developing this triathlon for German Shepherds which includes:

- Tracking
- Obedience
- Protection

It's also more than just a strictly judged competition sport. As part of the Schutzhund "degree," the individual dog is evaluated physically and mentally for his breeding suitability. IPO (International Pruefungsordnung) is a similar competition to Schutzhund.

Personal Protection

While there are many companies out there who will sell you a trained dog for personal protection, you can also have your own dog professionally trained if he has the right temperament. Or in theory you can train your own dog in personal protection, although I don't recommend that. If you don't know what you are doing you can end up with an extremely antisocial and aggressive dog that is not suitable for a family environment. So, if after extensive obedience train-

Photo Courtesy of Celeste Schmidt Dakonic GSDs

ing, you think your family still needs a higher degree of protection, see if your GSD would qualify for professional personal protection training.

Detection Dogs

When it comes to this category, most of us think of detection dogs as the drug-sniffing and bomb-searching hounds that you can see any night on a variety of television shows. While those pursuits are almost entirely in the hands of police and law enforcement agencies, there are a variety of detection services offered by civilian trainers and their dog partners.

- Termite detection. These destructive little insects use a variety of odors to communicate and that's where the GSD's incredible sniffer comes into play. Termite detection dogs are capable of signaling the presence of this bad bug even before the human eye can see any damage.

- Mold detection. Another property value destroyer that can be discovered by the educated GSD. As with any scent detection process, the dog is exposed to a variety of common molds and their smells, which then go into the canine's encyclopedic memory of odors.

- Accelerant detection. These specially trained dogs assist fire and police departments in the investigation of fires that have been intentionally set.

- Bed bug detection. While the thought of bed bugs in your house might make your skin crawl, for a well-trained canine bed bug sleuth, the idea of looking for these blood-sucking critters is exciting. A competent dog detective should be able to smell live bed bugs and eggs as well as old infestations.

- Conservation detection. These dogs are used to help conduct surveys in wildlife research by looking for scat and other signs of an animal's presence in a given geographical area.

So, these are the hard-core, rough-and-ready occupations that you and Boris could get involved in. Who knows, you might even be able to make a living out of one of them. Boris's Bed Bug Banishing Business Inc. Has a nice ring to it, I think. But if you are thinking that you'd like to do something with Boris that's more people orientated, something therapeutic maybe, how about this?

Therapy Dogs

This job is all about quality of life. Therapy Boris goes into retirement homes, hospitals, schools, anywhere he is invited. He brings a sense of comfort and companionship to people who sometimes just need to reach out and hug something. There are tests to pass in order to qualify, but the number one requirement is a capacity for calmness. Laidback Boris, good boy.

Service Dogs

There are three types of service dogs.

1. Guide dogs work with visually impaired people.
2. Hearing dogs help deaf and hearing-challenged individuals.
3. Service dogs work with people who have mobility issues, psychiatric challenges, and medical concerns.

While it is possible to acquire a fully trained dog from various disability-related organizations, the waiting lists are somewhat discouraging. Not to mention the twenty-thousand-dollar-plus price tag. You can train your own service dog, but it will take time and money. I suggest going to the American Kennel Club's website for more information on how to get started.

Photo Courtesy of Michele Hill

You can find details at: www.akc.org/expert-advice/training/service-dog-training-101/

Now, if you're looking for a dog occupation that thrives on pure energy, speed, and athleticism this next one might hit the spot. You need to be able to make split-second decisions, work with hand signals and voice commands, plus be able to beat the clock.

Agility Training

Photo Courtesy of Samuel Ireland

You and Boris will need to achieve a high level of obedience training in order to be successful on the agility course. The competitions include obstacles, tunnels, jumps, weave poles, and even a broad jump. It's all about teamwork and intensity.

If you want to compete but don't want to sprint around an agility course you could consider an activity that will have you doing a little jogging around the ring and it might even take you to the Big Apple and the Westminster Dog Show.

Conformation Training

Dog showing is one of the most popular competitive canine activities in the country. It's a contest where individual dogs are judged against specific breed standards. Here's how to get started if you have a hankering for the show ring.

- Make sure that your GSD is registered with the American Kennel Club.
- Join your local AKC club. They offer training classes.
- If you think your dog has great potential and you have deep pockets you can hire a professional handler for a fee.
- No spayed or neutered animals allowed.

Herding Training

The American Kennel Club recognizes three styles of competitive herding.

- In the A course, the dog is required to drive stock through a setting that includes gates and pens.

- The B course requires the dog to round up stock at some distance from the shepherd and bring them back.

- C course monitors the dog as it tends, patrols, and controls a flock or herd as it grazes, keeping the animals out of unwanted areas.

The AKC offers these trials and also tests to determine if your dog has the instinct to be a successful shepherd dog.

Obviously, there are many activities you and Boris could spend time bonding and burning calories. Sort of depends on your level of dedication and interest. But what if your dog seems to have some trouble understanding what you want her to do? What if she is exhibiting downright bad behavior? It could just be a reflection of everything you've taught her. That's where the trail takes us in the next chapter, called "Unwanted Behavior: Who's a Bad Girl?"

CHAPTER 14
Unwanted Behavior: Who's a Bad Girl?

The first thing you need to check on in any attempt to analyse and change your German Shepherd's behavior is the health of your dog. Is there a medical problem that is causing the action you are trying to change?

✔ By now you are on a first-name basis with your local veterinarian; they probably even keep an open slot for you at the clinic because they appreciate your business so much. Ear infection, bladder infection, you name it, get a clean bill of health from Dr. Feelgood before moving on to concocting a corrective course of action.

Providing your veterinarian has given you and Hermione (Her-my-oh-knee) the medical all-clear, the next step on your bad behavior checklist should be one of my usual suspects.

✔ Physical & Mental Exercise. If you aren't semi-exhausted trying to keep your GSD stimulated, then you're not doing your job. These dogs will occupy themselves if you don't supervise and when they keep themselves busy, destruction of property is not far behind.

So, you've concluded that Hermione is healthy; she's getting lots of physical exercise and you're playing chess with her every day so she is mentally stimulated. So why all the barking? And bad behavior goes way beyond barking. Let's look at my "who's a bad girl?" shopping list.

Who's a Bad Girl?

- Excessive barking and whining. GSDs are prone to bark at most things anyway but there is a limit. Excessive is when they exceed the average 10 barks a day.

- Lunging. We've all been there. It's very poor form to have your dog lunging at other dogs and various small animals.

- Bolting. This is a close second to lunging in my "bad girl" books. No one needs a runaway GSD in their lives.

- Jumping up. It's not acceptable and it could be downright dangerous.

- Chewing. And more chewing. Shoes, wallets, cell phones, anything can be fair game.

- Begging. It's irritating and it's got to stop. How did this start anyway?

*Photo Courtesy of
Makenzi Hall*

- Leash pulling. My favorite pet peeve. Really, what is the hurry?
- Mouthing. Many of you may know this by its other names: biting and nipping.
- Counter surfing. We've talked about this previously. It's the kind of clean sweep no one wants in their house.
- Self-mutilation. If you didn't raise this with your vet, it's time for another consult.
- Aggression. This can take many forms but always results in unwanted and sometimes dangerous behavior.

This is just my "who's a bad girl?" list and it is by no means exhaustive, but all of it can be exhausting nonetheless. Your next step in dealing with any one of these individual behaviors is to determine the root cause. That reminds me that digging isn't on the list but very well could be. Anyway, putting that aside for the moment, let's pluck at random from the list, one behavior to deal with as an example.

Photo Courtesy of
William Chilton

Bad Girls, What You Gonna Do?

Bolting. Imagine this scenario. You decide you need to go out the front door. Say, to pick up the newspaper lying on the front lawn. That's if you're lucky enough to still get newspaper home delivery. But just as you open the door you are knocked forcibly aside by a black and tan freight train on four legs on her way to freedom. That's bolting. She could just as easily have been charging out the back door, out of the car at the dog park or out the gate into heaven knows where. Bolting is not what I would describe as a psychiatric issue, a mental problem, but it is behavioral and needs fine tuning. It might be a training issue that you've ignored. Maybe you just had too much on your plate. Everyone in the house said they wanted a dog but when push comes to shove, Hermione seems to be your GSD. Especially when there's a problem. So, seeing as you own the bolting brain-teaser, here's what I would suggest in this case.

Interrupt Command

This is a useful directive to have in your training toolbox and it can be used to stop Hermione from bolting, dead in her tracks. In this case I want to talk about the "Wait" command. This interrupt command can be used to head off any number of undesirable behaviors, plus it has the double whammy effect of asserting your leadership, which is something you need to do at every turn. Why? Essentially because Hermione needs to know who is calling the shots in your household and it darn well better not be her.

Wait for Me

1. You will need to put Hermione on a leash. The leash is a psychological move as well as putting you in a position to physically restrain her. The mental aspect says "I am in control. Pay attention to me." It's part of you being a leader for your German Shepherd.

2. Position yourself at the door with Hermione beside you. You will sense the excitement in your dog so it's time to get ready to assert control.

3. Open the door. When Hermione lunges, give her a quick but firm pull on the leash, say "wait," and quickly close the door.

4. You'll need to do this repeatedly, tugging on the leash, saying the "wait" command, and shutting the door until, miracle of all miracles, you open the door one time and Hermione just stands there, hopefully looking at you.

5. When Hermione finally restrains herself, that calls for praise and treats.

6. You must continue to practice this until you can leave the door open and Hermione makes no move to bolt and simply waits for the next instruction from you.

7. You need to remember to do this each time you get ready to exit. Repetition makes it a desirable habit.

Mind Meld

I don't know how many original Star Trek fans are reading this but in that old TV series Spock was able to do something called the Vulcan mind meld. He would use telepathy to get into someone else's mind and essentially combine the two minds, creating a "mind meld." Why am I bringing this up in a book about German Shepherds? Well, from my experience it seems that every day my GSD plays mind meld games with me. If Cody could use telepathy on me the daily conversations would go something like this.

Cody: "Well, what are we going to do today? I'd like to go down this path right here, let me show you what I'm thinking. That black squirrel that I saw right here the last two days in a row might still be hanging around..."

Me: "No, we can't go down that path. We have to go over here because there's some brush I need to pick up and move to the burn pile."

Cody: "Oh man, not work, that's so boring. Why don't we skip that and go for a walk down by the well? That's where the rabbits hang out and I almost caught one the other day."

Me: "No, Cody. We have to move the brush. Right now."

Cody: "Whatever you say, but what about...."

I think you get the idea. German Shepherds are always pushing the envelope and when their behavior goes unchecked or unmonitored, they just assume that they have a stamp of approval because they are smart and confident individuals. They do want to work with their humans but it's not an unqualified relationship of total acceptance. You need to be the leader and creatively approach any problems with GSD behavior on several different levels.

Trigger Finger

Put your finger on any triggers for the behavior you are trying to change and eliminate them. Disconnect the doorbell, walk the other way if your GSD is tempted to mix it up with the oncoming dog, take the food off the counter. If you stop to think about triggers, you can eliminate most of them.

Double Exposure

Sometimes a stimulus, a trigger, can be overcome by exposure. If loud music or the radio sets your dog off, play it more often. The more it becomes a part of a dog's life, the more it becomes part of the passing scenery. Another trigger can be small children. Some German Shepherds just don't know what to make of them. They aren't sure if they are a toy, or possibly a small animal of some kind to be chased. You have to monitor this kind of a socialization situation carefully, but increasing exposure to small children, a little bit at a time, normalizes little people in your German Shepherd's eyes.

Ignorance Is Bliss

If Hermione is turning into a beggar of food scraps there are a couple of reasons for it. Opportunity and reinforcement. Both of those land squarely on your shoulders. Stop giving that begging face any table scraps and never do it again. Ignore the begging and whining until eventually it ceases. It will be a tug-of-war but you'll win in the end if you stay strong. Sometimes ignoring something will lead to bliss.

Multiple Choice

If your German Shepherd is being a bad girl, remember to divert and distract. Chewing on your favorite Manolo Blahnik party shoes? Hand over one of her favorite squeaky toys so she drives everyone crazy with that instead. If you introduce other options to your dog, she's an opportunist, she will take advantage of the next best thing.

Call in the Experts

"Nipping and biting can be a challenge to new German Shepherd owners. Understand that this is a breed bred for prey drive and herding. You will never change that instinct but can use the drive to teach other wanted behaviors."

Erika Martin
Century Farms

If you are still having difficulties with bad behavior after doing your best to eliminate it, then it is time to call in the troubleshooters. Trainers are most often brought in to deal with issues of aggression and separation anxiety. You just may be too close to the situation to work out a custom solution. It's a good leader who knows when to ask for help.

Good Girl, Good Boy!

There are solutions to many unwanted behaviors. That is, if you think about what the issue is, take into account Hermione's personality, and are willing to spend the time and, if need be, money. As we close this chapter out, I want to mention several of the breed-specific behavioral issues that I have found in my GSD experience.

- Barking. GSDs bark at everything. They will bark going into a room. They will bark at people coming into a room. I believe it is just in their nature to sound the alarm. You can stop excessive barking by using an interrupt command, but I don't use it often. Some barking is just part of the package.

- Separation anxiety. German Shepherds love their people and will spend all their time walking right on your heels everywhere you go, even into the bathroom if you don't shut the door. You must train them early to understand that when you leave, you always come back.

The last issue I want to raise is the minefield of aggression. The "A" word is a catchall for several types of behavior that have their own unique origins.

1. Dominance aggression. Usually directed toward family members. Shows itself in actions such as pushing through doorways and simply ignoring commands from people the dog feels it doesn't have to listen to.

2. Fear aggression. The German Shepherd may be afraid of people outside her own family, or of things she doesn't encounter often. Usually shows itself as growling, baring teeth, and barking.

3. Protective aggression. A GSD is inclined to be territorial and if experiencing this type of aggression will bark and growl, which can escalate to chasing and biting if the animal feels threatened.

These are the three main aggression categories and they all can be broken down into more specific sub-categories,

HELPFUL TIP
Doggy Care

Because German Shepherds are a highly intelligent breed, they can be easily bored, and a dog who is bored can be mischievous and sometimes destructive. If you work away from home, you may decide to explore options for your dog's care while you are away. Many cities now offer day-care services for dogs whose owners work. These facilities typically offer socialization, exercise, and entertainment for your dog. Keep in mind that there is currently no federal requirement for licensure for these establishments, so be sure to check that local permits and licensure have been acquired before signing your dog up.

tailored to the individual GSD. All of these problems, if they persist with your dog, are best handled by a professional trainer with a good reputation for positive results through positive reinforcement.

Let me end this chapter, where we have looked at so many negative aspects of these fine dogs, with a positive observation. There is nothing more satisfying at the end of a fun day than to look at your German Shepherd and say "Good girl!" or "Good boy!" because in the end, they truly are good dogs.

CHAPTER 15
The Open Road

"If you travel young and make it a normal part of the growing up, they will travel well forever. I recommend using a crate and make the crate a positive thing, then they can go anywhere in that crate. They just love their pack and want to be with them."

November Holley
Harrison K-9

I'm going to start off this section of The Complete Guide to German Shepherds with a slightly different approach to traveling with your GSD. In fact, I'm going to begin with a question. When you are getting ready to travel, ask yourself this.

- Where will your German Shepherd be the most comfortable?

We always need to consider what is best for our GSDs in any situation and traveling is no exception. Yes, your big boy is part of the family and he enjoys hanging out with everyone in the pack, but will he enjoy being packed into a crate and flown across the country? Will he actually get a kick out of the hotel rooms he'll be staying in?

I think you know where I'm going with this. Dogs and trips always need to be considered on an individual basis. And it's all right if you arrive at the decision that your German Shepherd would be better off staying home with a trusted caregiver. That would be the most sensible decision if your GSD gets too stressed by being uprooted. He'll miss you when you're gone but you won't take any years off his doggy life by making him pack his kibble for an extended trip when he'd rather just travel around the dog park. We'll come back to the various home stay options a bit later in this chapter. Now, with that very important consideration out of the way, let's move on to the rest of you who are thinking about hitting the open road.

My Tip
> Before you even think about hitting the road on a longer trip, make sure that your GSD has had lots of short-hop car travel experience. Every day if you can manage it. If your pup is prone to motion sickness, buy a dog seat belt that supports him facing forward instead of looking to the side. That will cut down on the upchuck.

Pre-Launch Preps

So, it's time for a road trip and everyone is really excited. People are packing way too much, everyone wants to bring their laptops and cell phones, and you just got the DVD player fixed in the van, so things are looking up. The suitcases are piling up but wait a second. What about Wolfgang? Who's packing for him?

Before You Leave the Driveway

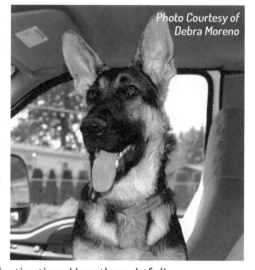

Photo Courtesy of Debra Moreno

- You've made reservations, right? All the hotels are dog-friendly right? Check for dog parks and other suitable exercise areas in the vicinity before booking.

- It just might be worth your while to make an appointment for Wolfgang with your vet for a quick checkup. What's that old line about an ounce of prevention?

- Someone has made a note of the nearest veterinarian offices or animal hospitals along the way and at your destination. How thoughtful!

- Make sure all Wolfgang's medical information and his meds are packed for the trip.

- Double-check that your dog's ID tags, with your contact information, are intact, legible, and attached securely to his collar.

- It's preferable that Wolfgang is microchipped. You can't lose an implant.

- Pack several recent pictures of your GSD. If he somehow gets lost, you'll want to be able to describe him complete with flattering photo.

- Make sure you've packed a leash, dog food, lots of water, food and water dishes, poop bags, brush, AND

- Dog first aid kit, which includes gauze, adhesive tape, scissors, tweezers, tick removal tool, antiseptic wipes, Benadryl, and a muzzle.

- Dog harness with tether. You want to make sure Wolfgang is secure in his seat and not roaming about the vehicle at will.

Photo Courtesy of Mark Hager

- Multiple rolls of paper towels. These come in handy for all kinds of family situations but work especially well for GSD emergencies.

- Pack a foldable traveling crate especially if your GSD is crate trained and will be looking for one to sleep in at night.

- Toys. His favorites and a couple of others. Can never have too many toys.

But wait a minute, now you're reconsidering the road trip. All those hours driving don't sound so attractive when you add up the stops and hotel stays and meals. You're thinking maybe you'll fly. You can just crate Wolfgang up, put him on the plane, pick him up at the other end, and away you go. All the fun of a holiday but no interstate inertia. Not so fast, though. You thought there were lots of GSD preparations for a road trip? Consider getting ready for lift-off.

Flight Plan

- Book a direct flight for Wolfgang. You know how you feel if you have too many stops. Imagine being a dog in a crate who has never flown before.

- Most airlines have pet shipping guidelines which you need to consult. Included in those is the requirement for a health certificate issued by a veterinarian.

- Make sure you have an approved shipping crate. Check with the specific airline you are using to confirm that your crate meets their specifications.

- The crate should be the same size as the one you use at home. If you don't crate your dog in the house and have to purchase one, make sure it is large enough for Wolfgang to stand up and turn around in. It should be well ventilated with an absorbent bottom.

- If your dog has not been crate-trained, get him used to the crate well before take-off day.

- The crate should be appropriately identified with your name and contact numbers as well as the dog's name.

- Before you leave for the airport make sure Wolfgang has had a reasonable amount of exercise. Being semi-exhausted will help take the edge of his flight anxiety.

- If you think Wolfgang might not travel well and are considering tranquilizing him, think twice. The AVMA (American Veterinary Medical Association) recommends you DO NOT tranquilize because it can cause heart and respiratory problems.

HELPFUL TIP
International Travel

If you're traveling internationally with your German Shepherd, it's important to check the rabies status of the country to which you are flying. The United States is classified as a rabies-controlled country. Travelling from a rabies-controlled country to a rabies-free country requires a rabies titer test (in addition to other documentation) and may also require a quarantine period. Hawaii is the only U.S. state that is rabies-free and therefore requires a quarantine in certain situations. Be sure to check regulations for your pets in advance for wherever you intend to travel.

One last note about air travel and German Shepherds. There is always a risk for animals when traveling by plane. Make sure your decision is well thought out and not a spur-of-the-moment choice.

Thinking Twice

So now having gone through all the preparations needed for taking Wolfgang on holiday with the family, you're thinking maybe he really would rather stay at home. But you haven't explored any of the options.

Kennel Considerations

Don't pick a kennel at random after Googling a bunch on the internet. Just because it's in the neighborhood, has a special offer of twenty-five percent off for a limited time, and provides free treats doesn't mean a darn thing. You spend lots of quality time at the vet's office. Why not see if they have any kennel recommendations? If they do, and if you can find clients of said kennel to talk to, that will give you the low-down and just maybe point you in the right direction. Intelligence gathering on your neighborhood walks or at the dog park is also a way to try and get a bead on a kennel. Once you have a few names in hand to think about, go and check them out.

*Photo Courtesy of
John Micallef*

Facility Focus

- How do you feel when you're walking around the grounds? You need to feel comfortable with the environment.

- What's the noise level? If it's excessive you should be thinking about somewhere else.

- Does it smell? This is always an indication of the sanitation level, or lack thereof, which can be indicative of not enough staff, not enough attention to detail.

- Does it seem crowded?

- German Shepherds need lots of exercise. How will they make sure Wolfgang gets his daily workouts?

- Make sure you see where the animals are kenneled overnight. I once asked to see that portion of a kennel that I was considering and when they wouldn't let me into that area, I crossed that place off my list immediately.

- Understand the kennel's fee structure, and if there are extras that you can opt for that will make for a better stay for your German Shepherd, consider them.

- Determine what vaccinations are required for boarding. A kennel at a minimum should mandate all dogs be up to date on rabies, distemper, and parvovirus as well as Bordetella.

- Does the kennel have a Facebook or other social media page where you can check out what is being said about the business?

- How well is the facility staffed? What about overnight?

- Wolfgang needs to stay on his regular diet so ensure that any kennel you are contemplating using will feed your GSD according to your instructions and with the food you provide.

- Find out what veterinary services are available. If your dog needs medical help ask if your own vet can be used.

- Once you've decided on a kennel, make sure you leave a local emergency contact name and number. This should be someone who can be immediately accessible when needed.

Finding the right facility is not a simple or easy process and you will have to invest some considerable research time to make sure you get it right. The other thing you need to consider if you're dead set on putting your GSD in a kennel while you're gone is doing a couple of trial stays before you go away for an extended period of time. One thing I did with Cody, my GSD, was take him to a boarding kennel just for the day to get him used to being at the particular location. Dogs love familiarity.

Home Stay

There are a couple of other vacation care options for Wolfgang that you should consider. I've always thought that keeping a dog in his familiar environment as much as possible lessens the anxiety associated with the owner's absence. Hiring a pet sitter might be the best option for some folks. You can even have the sitter come and stay in your home while you are gone. Let's look at some of the things you need to consider when looking for that perfect pal for your pet.

Finding the Right Fit

Photo Courtesy of Theresa Christ

You know you have to interview some candidates for the job. So, what are the qualifications you're looking for in someone who is going to take care of Wolfgang and stay in the family home? It's quite a personal assignment when you think about it. First of all, I would suggest that any sitter you are considering needs to have experience with bigger dogs and especially German Shepherds. GSDs aren't just another breed of dog and any potential sitter needs to understand what makes them tick. They're big, active, intelligent dogs, so hiring an older, more sedentary person might not be the best idea. Make sure any possible sitter is a dog person, not an all-rounder. Here's my suggested list of things to consider.

- Ideally the sitter will come and stay in your home. That way your GSD gets to maintain his normal routine.

- Are they insured and bonded? If they are, they are taking the business seriously, which increases your odds of dealing with a professional.

- What practical experience do they have? If they have had dogs of their own and been involved in training that's a bonus.

- Can they provide references and testimonials?
- Work out a daily schedule with the potential sitter. You need to determine if they can handle the demands a GSD will put on them.
- Make sure the person you are talking to is the person who will be looking after Wolfgang the whole time. Tag teaming with someone else is not acceptable.
- Are there add-on services that might be worth your while to purchase, such as grooming and training?
- Is the sitter familiar with the positive reinforcement style of dealing with a challenging pet?
- Ascertain the best way to stay in touch with the sitter while you're away. Text, email, phone call?
- Can you get updates while you're away?
- Lastly, be prepared for a series of questions from any good pet sitter. They will want to know as much as possible about you and your pet. That's also the sign of a professional.

Once you've narrowed your possible pet sitter list down to one you like, take them for a test drive. A weekend away will tell you if they're the one you can count on.

The Best for Last

I had an ulterior motive when I introduced my two-month-old GSP to the next-door neighbor. I hoped they would bond as Cody grew up, so my German Shepherd wouldn't become "that barking dog next door." And, sure enough, that's what happened. It didn't help that the neighbor had been bitten by a GSD as a paper boy, but today Cody and the neighbor are best-friends. Guess where Cody stays whenever my wife and I take a trip? Yep, with the guy next door. When I call this section "The Best for Last" I mean it. If you have a family member, friend, or good neighbor who can take care of your GSD while you're away, that is probably the best of all possible worlds. Chances are if the person pet sitting has a personal connection with Wolfgang, you know they will go the extra mile to make sure everything works out.

CHAPTER 16
A Dog's Breakfast

I'm standing in a local pet food store gazing up and down the aisles. There is dog food everywhere. Massive bags of dry kibble that most humans would need help loading into their cars. Endless shelves holding thousands of dog food cans with a dizzying array of colorful labels. And the information on those labels!

HELPFUL TIP
Pass the Pumpkin

Having an upset stomach can be just a regular part of life for your dog. However, there are times when an upset stomach can be a life-threatening issue, especially for puppies, so always make sure you assess the underlying cause of stomach problems with your vet. For nonserious stomach issues, many pet owners turn to canned pumpkin! While humans usually reach for saltines and ginger ale for an upset stomach, pumpkin's low glycemic index and slow absorption can help your dog with digestion and an uneasy stomach. Check with your vet to see how much pumpkin you should give based on your dog's size, and be sure not to use canned pumpkin pie mix; you don't want to feed your dog spices.

- Omega source
- Nutrient-rich with amino acids
- Grain free
- Contains no meat by-products, wheat, corn, soy
- Made in USA with globally sourced ingredients
- Cage-free chicken formula

If I was a first-time dog owner looking at all this, I would be dismayed and stunned. I was a first-time pet owner. I was dismayed and stunned. Putting together a nutritional diet for your German Shepherd doesn't need to be overwhelming and it doesn't need to cost an arm and a leg. You do need to be aware that if your German Shepherd doesn't get the proper balance of proteins, fats, and minerals, they can become unhealthy. Your dog depends on you. So, you need to ask, and answer, some basic questions in order to point you and your GSD in the right direction.

When you picked your puppy up on day one, the breeder had weaned Maggie and moved her onto some dry kibble food. That was just the breeder's choice of food and perhaps had as much to do with a pet food company's sponsorship as anything else. The same would go for whatever foods your veterinarian might recommend. The bottom line here is that whatever foods have been suggested to you might be perfectly fine, but what do you want to do?

What Is a Balanced Diet?

Put three German Shepherd owners in a room and you will get three different opinions on the best way to feed your GSD. So, here's what I'm going to do. I'll outline the options, tell you what I do, and then you can figure out the best way for Maggie to get her daily calories. And not just calories, but nutrition. Let's start with the basics.

Lap It Up

Maybe, just maybe, here's one aspect of diet that all dog people can agree on. Most of us don't give water much thought but when it comes to our dogs, H20 is crucial. GSDs are large dogs and obviously need more water than Aunt Paula's Pomeranian. You're looking at an adult GSD, moderately active, needing to drink about an ounce of water per pound of body weight per day. Hotter weather, more exercise, more water.

Aqua Advice

- Fresh water should always be accessible.
- Change it frequently.
- This might sound funny but urge your GSD to drink. They have a lot on their minds, and I think sometimes they just forget to lap it up. Remind them.

The Basic Diet

"Most German Shepherds do great on a balanced commercially available dog food. Some dogs can have food allergies or special dietary requirements, but choosing a well bred dog should prevent most of these issues."

Katie Halfen
Casamoko Shepherds

So here we go, back to standing in the pet food store, gazing at the endless rows of pre-packaged canine calories. If you decide to feed your GSD strictly store-bought food, most commercial brands are formulated to provide the basic nutrients that Maggie will need. Many will say that they meet the nutritional guidelines set out by the AAFCO (Association of American Feed Control Officials). These are model standards established for informational purposes and have no regulatory role. Regulation is handled by the various states and the Federal government. Canned food will usually outline its contents in two ways.

- Ingredients
- Guaranteed analysis

If you're a label reader watch for something like the following in the ingredients list. Say you have one can each of two equally expensive, chicken-based dog food. One company lists the number one ingredient as boneless chicken. The other notes the first ingredient as chicken broth. Which one should you take home? I would suggest the one that lists boneless chicken off the top is probably a better bang for your buck. Read the fine print.

Canned food, or wet food as it's also called, can be all you feed your GSD but unless you are supplementing Maggie's diet in other ways, with bones, for example, her teeth won't get the workout they need to stay relatively clean. I combine wet food and a kibble for most of Cody's meals. The thinking there is that the kibble will provide some of the abrasive action needed to remove the tartar that can build up on a dog's teeth.

All those bags of dry food, or kibble, advertise themselves in much the same way as the canned food but upon examination you'll find the kibble much less appetizing when you read the ingredients. Dry food

manufacturers also tout meeting AAFCO nutritional levels; for instance, the one I have in front of me lists corn as the number one ingredient followed by chicken by-product meal and then brewers rice. Dry food also lists the guaranteed analysis. That analysis might look something like this.

✔ Crude protein 23%

✔ Crude fat 15%

✔ Crude fiber 3.9%

✔ Moisture 10%

You do need to do some research and read the fine print but here are some general nutritional guidelines to follow with pre-packaged dog food.

- Protein should be the number one listed ingredient and be identified as a whole meat such as beef, chicken, or fish. Protein goes toward muscle building and maintenance.

- Fat is needed in your German Shepherd's diet. It helps promote a healthy coat and skin. It can also be problematic for some GSDs. While the levels of fat in wet and dry food are generally not a concern, GSDs can have difficulty digesting fat, so if you supplement Maggie's diet, best to stay away from any fatty foods.

- Vegetable and fruits. Most dogs will continue to eat what they have been introduced to as puppies. That why carrot-consuming, apple-eating, broccoli-chewing dogs are not uncommon. These foods also give them a whole bunch of minerals and vitamins they wouldn't otherwise get in that form. Veggies and fruit are good for the animal's digestion and elimination processes.

Rounding out my thoughts on the store-bought menu option, one of the major drawbacks is expense. You do quite often get what you pay for in this retail realm so the better food for Maggie will also probably be the most expensive.

A Raw Deal

Here's another approach to feeding your German Shepherd. A growing number of dog owners have their pups on a raw food diet. There are different ideas about how to achieve this but here's the main thrust: dogs are carnivores and their systems are designed to consume raw meat and bones. What does this diet look like? Here it is, at its most basic.

Prey Model Raw Food Diet
- 80% muscle meat
- 10% edible bones
- 5% liver
- 5% other organ meat

Some GSD owners tweak this diet even further. They follow something called the Franken Prey diet. They assemble meats and parts from various animals and birds, believing that it's healthier to have some variety of "prey" protein. There is a third group of owners who feed their German Shepherds "whole prey." This entails feeding the entire prey animal at one time. The concept here is that everything is natural and in balance coming from that single item on the menu. Some raw feeders will add Omega 3 to their animals' diets, believing commercial meats lack that fatty acid.

Raw Philosophy
- Raw is natural
- Plant matter is not needed for carnivores
- Supplementation should be limited

There is no such thing as the status quo in the dog world and diets are no exception. While we've talked about a strict raw diet for German Shepherds portraying dogs as natural carnivores, there is another group of owners who think that dogs are naturally omnivores. Meat and plant eaters. Feeding dogs adhering to this philosophy is known as the BARF diet. Not what I would have called it, but anyway.

BARF Believers

BARF stands for Biologically Appropriate Raw Food. I don't want this whole chapter to be about raw but I would be remiss if I didn't mention this style of diet. Where the BARF people differ from the strictly raw meat feeders is that the menu is a little more wide-open.

- In addition to meat and bones, the BARF diet includes 10% vegetables, fruits, seeds, and nuts. Proponents also suggest that any veggies or fruit be steamed or pureed to help the dog's digestion.

What's That You're Eating?

It's a question we all have to contend with when those big Shepherd eyes are staring us in the face at mealtime. Do you let Maggie eat people food? Well, I can tell you there are some foods that humans regularly consume that are poisonous for dogs. Let's go down that list right now.

Do Not Feed the Animals

- Chocolate & Caffeine (that includes cocoa powder and baker's chocolate)
- Grapes & Raisins
- Onions
- Alcohol
- Hops (found in beer)
- Macadamia nuts
- Walnuts
- Avocado
- Xylitol (an artificial sweetener found in a variety of candy, baked goods, and some peanut butters)
- Cooked bones (they can be a splintering hazard)
- Fatty foods, including bacon and fat trimmings (they can cause pancreatitis)
- Apple seeds (they contain small amounts of cyanide)

Everybody loves a home-cooked meal, German Shepherds included. You don't have to feed them table scraps; you can actually plan their menus and provide them with good-quality sustenance, food that you know is beneficial for them because you prepared it. I haven't advanced to the stage of complete meal planning for Cody, but I do buy meat at the supermarket and cook it to be mixed in with his regular canned food and kibble. If you decide to take on the responsibility of cooking for your GSD, you need to have a nutrition plan in place. Some veterinarians might be able to help you with this, but it might be a better idea to try to find someone specializing in canine nutrition.

You can make a start on feeding Maggie a better diet by adding to a store-bought menu. Here's a sample list of some foods to think about, and remember, German Shepherds love real meat. I always look for the bargain protein that is priced for same day sale and either cook it when I get home or freeze it for later preparation.

- ✔ Ground beef or cubed stewing beef
- ✔ Liver (occasionally)
- ✔ Tuna & salmon

Photo Courtesy of Eduardo De Luna

- ✔ Chicken
- ✔ Boiled pasta. This can be entertaining watching strings of spaghetti hanging out of your German Shepherd's mouth. OK, it's quiet around my house sometimes.
- ✔ Cooked eggs
- ✔ Rice & potatoes
- ✔ Steamed vegetables

I reserve cheese for treats in small quantities. Cody has a rubberized treat bone with holes in each end that he drags around the house in the evenings looking for a peanut butter handout. He gets a few dabs most nights. There are a million recipes for homemade dog food on the internet, but you always need to put your nutritional template over any recipe before firing up the stove.

Back to those big German Shepherd eyes staring at you during dinner. You know, it's all right to feed dogs some table scraps as long as you're bearing in mind their health requirements. I suggest putting anything like that in Maggie's bowl for her to consume. You don't want to hand feed from the table and end up with a perpetual beggar. The other concern to have in mind is your dog's weight.

Weight Watchers

If you watch your German Shepherd's weight from day one you stand a better chance of winning any battle of the bulge that might have to be fought. Same sort of idea when it comes to your own waistline.

Fat Facts

- The adult obesity rate in America runs at about 33%. That's one in three people.
- Most studies put the canine obesity rate at 50%. That's a staggering one in two dogs.

From those heavyweight numbers you can see that what we are doing to ourselves, we are also inflicting on our dogs. And that's not fair. There is a pretty standard formula for overweight GSDs.

> Overfeeding + Lack of Exercise = Obesity

That formula doesn't take into account any medical problems Maggie might be experiencing. If your German Shepherd is gaining weight and your lifestyle hasn't changed substantially, the first resort, as I've said over and over again, is a medical once-over at your vets to rule out a physical problem.

If you have an overweight dog on your hands and you've zeroed in on the culprit, otherwise known as the "man in the mirror," then you can take steps to slim things down. One thing German Shepherd owners have going for them is that GSDs, on the whole as a breed, typically don't have a weight problem. How can you tell if your dog is overweight?

- Head to your vet's office and get Maggie to hop onto the scale. That will give you a baseline weight.
- Check with the vet for your dog's ideal weight.
- On average, GSDs weigh between 66 and 88 pounds.
- Take a look at your dog from the side. Does she have a waistline? If the waist doesn't tuck in, there's a weight problem.
- Run your hands over her ribcage from front to back. If you can't feel ribs that's another warning sign.

Stepping Up

You know the way to your vet's office. You could drive there in your sleep. On one of your trips do a consult with her about developing a weight loss plan for Maggie. Your vet will consider the age, overall health, and the number of pounds that should be dropped and help you develop a daily and gradual approach to better health for your GSD. It will establish a calorie limit per day. That plan might involve gradually changing some of the food you've been providing. It could also alter the way Maggie has been eating.

Chow Times

- If you've been a free choice feeder, that will probably have to change. Free choice means food available all the time with the dog choosing when and how much to eat.

- It's best to establish a feeding schedule. Two meals a day is the conventional approach with the portions strictly regulated.

- Your vet may also suggest a timed feeding approach. That requires placing the food down for a set period of time, say thirty minutes, and then taking it up at the end of that time.

- Treats may be something you want to eliminate or drastically scale back.

- If you've been supplementing Maggie's diet with human meal leftovers, you'll have to scrap that practice.

   Remember that overweight formula mentioned earlier?
   ➢ Overfeeding + Lack of Exercise = Obesity

You and the veterinarian will have nailed the overfeeding part of the equation. Now it's time for you and your GSD to implement the exercise portion. Weight loss, as you know, should be a gradual process. And you need to be consistent in your approach. If you've been thinking about dropping a few pounds you could make it a team effort and develop an exercise program that will benefit both you and your German Shepherd.

Easy Does It

- Start your exercise program gradually. Several fifteen-minute walks (say three to start) a day. Maybe throw in a little fetch time but don't overdo it.

- As you and Maggie start to become shadows of your former selves, you can pick up the pace. I would aim to ultimately be exercising for a couple of hours a day. That can be a combination of walks, ball throwing, tug-of-war, hide and seek, and whatever else you can think of to get moving.

- Swimming. If you can get your GSD in the water, and most of them love it, that is one great exercise that is relatively easy on the body, especially the overweight body. Moderation is key.

Maybe, just maybe, some of you are thinking, "You know, this all sounds great, but I just don't have the time to do all this. Losing weight is a full-time occupation and I already have a job." Well, consider these ideas.

- ✔ Get other family members to split the exercise time with you.

- ✔ Contribute to your local economy. Hire a dog walker to take Maggie out and hoof it around the block.

- ✔ Indoor workouts. Even getting your German Shepherd to go up and down the stairs a few times will contribute to burning some calories.

- ✔ If you live close enough, come home for lunch, and a walk.

- ✔ If you don't live close enough to come home at lunch, can you take your GSD to work with you? Your break times could be Maggie's break times.

- ✔ A visit to the dog park or to a canine buddy's back yard can be good for a romp.

If you get your GSD back to a healthy weight, you'll be keeping her healthier longer, increasing her life expectancy, and best of all giving her a better quality of life. Doesn't every German Shepherd deserve that?

My Tip
> *"If your dog is fat, you're not getting enough exercise."*

Unknown author

Now that you've got your GSD looking as sleek as a racing Greyhound, you'll need to think about having them irresistibly groomed. I have to confess, my wife keeps our German Shepherd looking his best, and it pays off. Just the other day when Cody and I were in the parking lot outside the pet food store, a man stopped and looked at my GSD and said, "Beautiful!" This can happen to you too, if you keep on top of all the brushing and clipping that needs to be done. You've got an appointment to visit the Shepherd Salon for some beauty tips in the next chapter.

CHAPTER 17
Shepherd Salon

"Shedding can be different for dogs depending on whether or not they are spayed or neutered. In fact GSD's shed twice a year normally, but dogs that have been fixed may seem to shed a lot more frequently. I believe diet, and stress, also play a role in shedding."

Doreen Metcalf
Timber Ridge Farm

Photo Courtesy of
Marisa McEachern

Sometimes people think grooming a German Shepherd is all about brushing them. While that's certainly an important part of the dog maintenance package, it's only one piece. We'll deal with all the other aspects of keeping your GSD healthy, like bathing, teeth brushing, and nail clipping in this chapter, but let's start things off with the beautiful double coat that comes as standard equipment on German Shepherds.

I have to laugh sometimes when I'm reading through various online dog forums and see the question "How can I stop my German Shepherd from shedding?" There's a pretty simple answer to that somewhat innocent query. You can't stop them shedding. That's why they are lovingly called "German Shedders." There are some things you can do to make their hair loss manageable, but you will never be without the odd tumbleweed of hair rolling through the house. Or the "is that a hair in my mouth?" moment. You might have seen the little signs in touristy shops that read something like this.

"In our house dog hair is both a condiment and a fashion accessory."

There may be some humor there but it's also a German Shepherd fact. Take it from me, with a good vacuum cleaner and consistent habits on your part, it's all manageable. There are some things you'll need to do, and if you make them daily chores, you will lessen your overall workload.

German Shedders

When you bring a German Shepherd home you are getting twice the hair for your money. Bet most people don't know that there are two coats on every GSD:

1. A top coat, the one that is visible to the naked eye. This is where the longer guard hairs grow and they are shed individually. This coat protects the dog's skin from moisture and dirt.

2. An undercoat, which is relatively dense with short hairs and is frequently shed in clumps. This coat keeps GSDs warm in cold weather and cooler in hot weather.

My Tip
> Never shave your German Shepherd. While some people might think it will make them cooler in hot weather, in fact without the moderating effect of his double coat the dog becomes susceptible to sunburn and even heatstroke.

Deal With It

One of the ways of keeping Crash's shedding under control is to brush him every day. That way you'll be collecting the loose hair gradually. A health concern that can arise from infrequent brushing is matting in the undercoat; that can lead to skin irritation and infections. I suggest you approach the brushing sessions as fun time with your pet. I have never known one of Cody's brushing sessions not to turn into a bit of a wrestling match complete with groaning and half-hearted attempts to get away. And that's just my wife's reaction when she brushes the dog. Another thing to get used to is that a GSD "blows" his coat twice a year. And that "blows" term is not used lightly. This happens once in the fall, bringing on a heavier coat for winter, and early in the spring, losing the winter coat in anticipation of the fun and frolic in warmer temperatures. You will be able to fill garbage bags full of GSD hair over those heavy shedding weeks.

Tools of the Trade

"I like to use a simple grooming rake and a slicker brush. This combo works great, the rake will take out the dead undercoat and the slicker helps finish it off. A high powered dog blow dyer is also fantastic for getting out loose coat. Just get ready, it will go flying!"

Celeste Schmidt
Dakonic German Shepherds

There are several items that will make your life a whole lot easier when it comes to giving Crash a stunning coiffure.

- Undercoat rake. This looks like a long-toothed comb with a brush handle and it enables you to get to the thick undercoat. Using it on your dog is kind of like giving them a massage and they will come to love it.

- Grooming comb. This is a steel comb which enables you to give specific areas a finer comb-out.

- Pin brush. This is a very gentle brush and is used mainly for dealing with the top coat. They can be two-sided, with shorter and longer pins on opposing sides.

Remember to be gentle when brushing. If you have a plush-coated or long-coated GSD remember to pay special attention to the tail and tops of the feet. The long hair on the top of the feet and between the toes can become matted very easily if neglected. If you are consistent with your daily brushing it can be completed in ten minutes. Like all routines for German Shepherds, once they become accustomed to the maintenance session it should go off without a hitch. The other thing I would remind you to do is talk to your German Shepherd while doing any kind of activity with them. They will listen endlessly to you, and rarely talk back.

The Infrequent Bather

German Shepherds don't need require very many baths. In fact, the rule around our house is that Cody doesn't usually get washed unless he smells so doggy that it's embarrassing. The theory behind that is not to wash away the coat's essential oils that help keep the fur healthy and the skin from drying out.

- When you do bathe your GSD, make sure to use a dog shampoo. Most of them have a neutral pH designed for a dog's skin.

- Look for one that contains natural ingredients and moisturizers. We use one that contains oatmeal.

- If your German Shepherd has a skin condition, it's best to see a vet for any medicated shampoo that may be required.

It's important to mention here that if your dog has a skin problem it could be directly related to the food he is consuming. Crash may have allergies, and a change in diet could be the key to alleviating any dermal distress. Feeding your GSD high-quality food will also ensure a healthy coat and skin.

Trimming Tips

Many people are intimidated by the thought of clipping their dog's toenails. In fact, I know people who go to one of the big box pet stores or their vet every time a pawdicure is required. If you start when your German Shepherd is a puppy and make sure you have a pair of good-quali-

Photo Courtesy of
Celeste Schmidt
Dakonic GSDs

ty nail clippers you can handle the job yourself. Your dog may never like getting his toenails trimmed but GSDs will learn to tolerate it.

- You will need to cut Crash's toenails on a regular basis. Checking them every week is a good thing. If you hear a clicking sound on the hardwood floor when your dog is walking around it's time.

- Trim a little bit each session. Many German Shepherds' toenails are black and you won't be able to see where the quick begins. The quick is a small area of blood supply and nerves to the toenail. If you accidentally cut that it will bleed.

- Make sure to have some kind of styptic powder on hand to stop the bleeding if you make a mistake.

- Don't forget the dewclaws. They are located on the inside of each paw.

Dental Design

As your puppy has been growing up you probably have been spending a lot of time avoiding his mouth. All that chewing and nipping can be tiresome after a while. Now I'm going to say that you need to pay special attention to Crash's teeth. Bone chewer or not, dental chew consumer or not, your dog is still going to need help with his oral hygiene. Just as in humans, if you don't deal with the plaque now, you will surely deal with it later.

- If you haven't bothered with your German Shepherd's teeth and need to have them professionally cleaned it can cost as much as eight hundred dollars. Your dog may also have to undergo general anaesthesia for the procedure. You don't want to go there.

Start with your German Shepherd early in his life and get him used to the fact that you are going to be poking things in his mouth, including your fingers. Whatever tool you decide to use you just need to get in there.

- ✔ There are all kinds of canine toothbrushes on the market. Some have angled bristles which may help with a deeper brushing.

- ✔ You can even get a brush that fits over your fingertip if you think that might work better for you.

- ✔ Dog dental wipes are available. Some of them are made using baking soda so it's a fairly natural way of cleaning Crash's teeth.

- ✔ Use canine toothpaste only. All kinds of flavors including our house favorite, peanut butter.

✔ You can use baking soda instead of toothpaste if you can get your dog to play along.

✔ Another way to spend your hard-earned cash and help with your German Shepherd's plaque is to offer him dental chews. Many of them claim to cure bad breath. I'll let you be the judge of that.

✔ Just a reminder. Dry food, kibble, provides some abrasive action on your dog's teeth.

You can brush your German Shepherd's teeth in a couple of minutes once Crash understands the program. I suggest brushing at the end of the day when your GSD is tired and his resistance may not be as strenuous.

● Spend your time on the outside of the teeth, which is where most of the plaque accumulates.

● Concentrate on the upper teeth for the same reason.

● Ideally hold your brush at a 45-degree angle and use circular strokes.

● No rinsing required.

Let me end this section with a statistic from the American Veterinary Dental College.

By three years of age most dogs have some evidence of periodontal disease.

Your dog doesn't have to be one of the unlucky ones. If you set a minimal goal of brushing three times a week that's probably not biting off more than you can chew.

The Eyes Have It

A German Shepherd's eyes and his vision are definitely some of nature's wonders. For starters, GSDs are not colorblind. They can see many shades of gray, blue, and yellow. Red and green not so much. They have great night vision and a much wider field of vision than we do, enabling German Shepherds to track moving objects better than humans.

Fortunately, German Shepherds have relatively few vision problems. You might see the odd bit of mucus in the corner of his eye from time to time but it's nothing that a quick wipe with a clean, damp cloth can't fix. If you detect anything beyond a little mucus, don't hesitate to pay your vet a visit.

*Photo Courtesy of
Tricia Ansell*

Play It by Ear

Checking Crash's ears is an integral part of the GSD grooming process. The ears will get dirty just from the usual daily wear and tear especially during the summer. There is an ear cleansing solution available from your vet that you can use for maintenance. Just squeeze some of the liquid on a clean cotton ball and swab out the inside of the ear.

- The big villain as far as a German Shepherd's ears are concerned is water. If Crash goes swimming and gets water in his ears that's a potential problem. The water changes the pH balance in the ear and can set the stage for infection. We use the vet-supplied ear cleansing solution in Cody's ears following every swim now after going through an ear infection.

- An indication that Crash is having an ear problem is lots of head shaking and ear scratching. If that carries on for a while it should call for a vet visit.

Your German Shepherd's ears should be given the once-over weekly. The ear solution is relatively inexpensive and should always be kept on hand. It can save you a lot of grief. The good thing about a Shepherd's upright ears is it makes them less susceptible to problems compared to the floppy-eared breeds.

Coming up in the next chapter we'll deal with some basic health care issues for your GSD. We'll cover many of the pests and diseases that you can encounter. But don't worry, I won't just give you problems, I'll provide some solutions too.

CHAPTER 18
GSD Basic Health Care

L et's go back to square one with this whole dog business. Well, maybe square two. Square one would be, you bring Schatzi home. Square two is you need to find a vet for Schatzi. Well, hold on a second, why do you need to find a veterinarian? There is a school of thought among some dog owners that veterinarians as a group, while providing an essential service and doing good work, are asking to see dogs and other animals too frequently. And during those frequent visits are over-prescribing tests, vaccinations, and medication. The reason behind this thinking is the supposition that vets are doing this because it's a long-es-tablished way of boosting their incomes. I'm not going to spend much time on this way of thinking but I did want to bring it to your attention. As I've said before, research is a German Shepherd owner's best friend when it comes to figuring out what is right for you.

Here's what I will say about the "too much vet" theory. Everyone gets to decide how often and for what reasons they go to the vet's office. But I don't think anyone wants to take chances with their dog's health.

AKC Recommendations

Here is a list of vaccines the American Kennel Club suggests for your German Shepherd.

1. Distemper
2. Measles
3. Parainfluenza

4. Rabies
5. Hepatitis
6. Parvovirus

In addition, there are optional vaccines available and recommended depending on where you live geographically.

1. Bordetella
2. Coronavirus

3. Lyme Disease
4. Leptospirosis

After the series of puppy vaccinations throughout the first sixteen months, the AKC recommends DHPP (distemper, hepatitis, parvovirus, and parainfluenza) and rabies shots every one to three years depending on what you and your vet opt for.

Vaccinosis

While talking about vets, I would be remiss in this section of the book if I didn't mention something called vaccinosis. This is a condition that is generally not mentioned by traditional veterinarians. Vaccinosis is a chronic condition that seems to arise from vaccinations. The symptoms can range from fever and hair loss to the more severe such as cancer and seizures. These symptoms don't typically show themselves until long after multiple vaccinations have been given. There are some holistic veterinarians who are very knowledgeable about vaccinosis so if you are concerned about the possibility with your dog it would be best to consult with a vet who believes that unnecessary vaccination can create chronic illnesses.

So, regardless of what vaccination regimen you decide on, you do need to have an ongoing relationship with your veterinarian. Ordinary things are going to come up. Ear infections, diarrhea that won't go away, hotspots that won't heal, the list is almost endless. On top of that I am going to recommend an annual visit for a Schatzi checkup, even if you think things are fine. At the very least during that yearly ritual, you can weigh your German Shepherd and have some trained, professional eyes go over your dog. The price of admission to the vet's office buys you some peace of mind. It's also called preventative health care. I call it a good idea.

What's Bugging You?

One of the least desirable things about owning a German Shepherd is the uninvited companions she may bring home on occasion. By that I mean something like, oh say, fleas. It's making me itchy just writing that word. Fleas are more than just pests. The little bloodsuckers are a bona fide health hazard.

Fleas Disease

This actually is where a good grooming routine can nip a potentially serious problem in the bud. You know about a Shepherd's double fur coat, we've talked about that already. It's the undercoat that is of concern here. The undercoat is for fleas, like the Hole in the Wall hideout was for Butch Cassidy and the Sundance Kid in the Wild West. Once the fleas are hidden in there it's hard to get them out. So, if you are brushing and combing your German Shepherd's coat out regularly you should be able to spot evidence of a flea infestation early, like flea feces, which look like little black flecks, or the little beggars themselves. Fleas are tiny but are visible to the naked eye and they will jump if you spot them. If you see them or signs of them here is what you need to do.

Flea Finale

You have to attack fleas on several different fronts but let's start with the dog. If you see your GSD doing a lot of chewing, scratching, and biting, chances are you and Schatzi are hosting a flea party.

- Use a flea shampoo on your GSD. This will get the insects out of the way, at least temporarily.

- You then need to get some long-term protection for Schatzi. You have a few different options. There are the topical treatments like Advantix or Frontline, which are applied by gloved hand to the back of the dog's neck. Products like Bravecto and NexGard come in a chewable tablet that lasts for one to three months. There are also some reasonably effective flea collars on the market. Your choice should be based on what you find works.

- You should consider spraying your yard with an insecticide to eradicate any existing population of fleas.

- If the infestation has been going on for some time, chances are the insects have also taken up residence in your house. The flea life cycle is such that even if you have killed off the adults there are eggs and larvae just waiting for their turn to make your life miserable. You'll then need to treat the inside of your home.

Deterring Disease

I mentioned that fleas are a health hazard and here's why. The little parasites can cause big trouble for your German Shepherd if left unchecked.

- Infections. The insects bite and bite and bite. Your dog will nip and chew and scratch, creating open sores which give nasty bacteria access to do their dastardly business.

- Dermatitis. Some German Shepherds are allergic to flea bites. This allergic reaction leads to skin infections.

- Tapeworms. Sends shivers down my spine just thinking about this one. Dogs naturally bite any fleas they can reach and sometimes eat them. If Schatzi ingests a flea that is infected with a tapeworm then she is in trouble.

- Plague. Flea bites can transmit this illness to your dog if the fleas have come in contact with an infected wild animal.

- Anemia. German Shepherds can suffer from a low red blood cell count which brings about severe fatigue if flea bitten too many times.

Tick Talk

Ticks are a much more serious threat to your dog than fleas. The various kinds of ticks are tiny and when you do spot them, if you examine them under a magnifier they look like a slow-moving, ugly spider. They may be small, but they can cause a host of problems for your German Shepherd if not dealt with. Ticks, like fleas, are also looking to suck blood from your dog but in exchange they leave behind a variety of debilitating illnesses. It's not a fair trade.

Telltale Tick Signs

Ticks are devious. I don't know what kind of a little brain they have in there, but you will find them when and where you least expect it. They range throughout most of the United States so there is no getting away from the little arachnids. They can't jump onto your dog. Instead they lounge on things like longer blades of grass and catch a ride on Schatzi when she brushes by. Here's how to tell if ticks are crawling around your neighborhood.

HELPFUL TIP
Hot Spots

Some dog breeds, including German Shepherds, are more susceptible to developing hot spots. These red, itchy lesions are caused by a dog repeatedly licking the affected area, causing irritation and inflammation. When diagnosing and treating hot spots, your vet will want to determine the underlying cause for the dog's behavior in order to prevent the hot spots from recurring. Possible causes are:

- Allergies
- Irritants
- Infections
- Stress
- Boredom
- Environmental factors

- You can actually see them. I have found them crawling on my clothing and the odd time on the floor. They look like a tiny dot but they will move slowly, looking for a place to sink their teeth in. If you see one in the house it will have probably ridden in on your dog.

- When you are brushing your GSD, you might run across what seems like a small bump on your dog's skin. A closer examination is called for. It could be an attached tick who is still feeding.

- If Schatzi is doing a lot of licking or chewing you need to take a closer look. If you see what looks like a scab, again it could be a tick.

- If your German Shepherd doesn't have much of an appetite and seems just a bit off, she could have a fever related to a tick bite. A key defense against ticks is regular, close examination of your dog.

- An attached tick will continue to feed, slowly increasing in size until they become as big as a small fingernail.

There are several suggested ways for removing ticks but one thing to keep in mind is never try to use your bare fingers. Squeezing a tick could send more toxic material into your dog's system. Ticks have a one-piece body so when removing them it's important to make sure you don't tear them apart and leave the mouth embedded in your GSD.

- You can use a blunt point pair of tweezers. Grasping the tick with the tweezers as close to your dog's skin as possible, gently pull upward in a straight continuous motion.

My Tip

➢ We've had good success in our house using something called a tick removal hook. It looks something like a mini prybar. With this handy little tool, you put the prongs on either side of the tick and twist, while pulling upward.

168

Just so you take any tick you run into seriously, here are some of the complications they can introduce into your dog's life if they get a chance. And not just your dog's life. The CDC (Centers for Disease Control and Prevention) reported almost sixty thousand human cases of tickborne disease in 2017.

Tickborne Disease

1. Lyme Disease. Symptoms include lack of appetite, lethargy, joint pain, and lameness. Antibiotics may be effective in dealing with the symptoms.
2. Rocky Mountain Spotted Fever. Fever, skin lesions, joint pain, and vomiting. Antibiotics may help.
3. Canine Ehrlichiosis. Fever, loss of appetite, nose bleeds. Again, antibiotics are prescribed.
4. Canine Anaplasmosis. Aside from fever, vomiting, and diarrhea, dogs may suffer seizures. Antibiotics suggested.
5. Canine Hepatozoonosis. Fever, muscle pain, bloody stools. Can be often fatal. Antibiotics are used to combat this nasty illness.
6. Canine Bartonellosis. Fever and lameness. If not treated the dog may develop heart or liver disease. Antibiotics need to be considered.
7. Canine Babesiosis. Anemia and vomiting. Antibiotics are on the agenda here for treatment.

Worms and Parasites

Almost all dogs will have worms during their lives. In fact, most puppies start their lives with them and have to be wormed multiple times in their young lives. Here are some of the little parasites that can worm their way, literally, into your German Shepherd's life.

- Roundworms. These little animals can be found in dogs of any age. Puppies can get them from their mothers and adults can pick them up from lying on infected soil or consuming a small animal, like a mouse that is infected. Many dogs show no sign of infection and a stool sample analysed by your vet can determine if they are present. Treatment consists of worming medication given by mouth. These parasites can also infect humans.

- Hookworms. These intestinal parasites take up residence in your German Shepherd's digestive system. They live in many types of soil and can infect your dog on contact. Because these worms are bloodsuckers, they can leave your pet with diarrhea and cause them to lose weight. De-worming medication is prescribed.

- Tapeworms. They are pests that attach to the intestines of the dog. You may find evidence of them around the anal area. They can look like grains of rice. Remember the flea advice earlier this chapter. If you run a flea-free operation you reduce your chances of Schatzi becoming a host to this menace. Oral medication is prescribed.

- Whipworms. They live in your dog's intestines. Whipworm larvae can be found in canine feces or surrounding soil. Cleaning up regularly after your dog will limit whipworm opportunity. Medication is available.

- Heartworms. These potential killers live in your pet's heart and lungs and are transmitted by mosquitoes. Adults can measure a foot or more in length. Fatigue and shortness of breath are signs of infection. Heartworm can be fatal. There are monthly pills and monthly topical medications that can be administered. There are medications available that deal with multiple worm threats at the same time.

Parasites Continued

At the risk of depressing you completely, I need to mention a few more threats to your German Shepherd's health. Remember, it's better to know about what you might have to deal with than be taken by surprise. It's doubtful that with careful and conscientious care your dog will encounter many of these annoyances. Still with me? OK, just a few more, I promise.

Photo Courtesy of Amy Fusco

- Giardia. A tiny parasite that lives, yes, you guessed it, in your dog's intestine. My dog, Cody, has been infected a couple of times because he insists on drinking pond water sometimes when I'm not watching carefully enough. Usually diarrhea is the outcome of this infection. Vet-prescribed drugs taken for about two weeks should clean things up.

- Ear Mites. Little pests that can plague your dog's ears. You might see what looks like a dark-colored ear wax like substance in the ears that can become raw and inflamed looking. Ear mites are contagious. Persistent scratching is a clue to their presence. Topical medication is available and regular cleaning of the ears is a must.

- Scabies. A mite that burrows into the skin which causes the dog to itch compulsively. Scratching leads to tearing the skin and scabs form. Patchy hair loss is also a symptom. Very contagious if animals are close contact. Clipping the fur may be required to treat. Medicated shampoo and oral medication could be prescribed.

- Coccidia. Another intestine-dwelling parasite. Dog feces and contaminated soil are the culprits for transference. Bloody diarrhea is a result of infection. Your vet can prescribe medication.

Spay, Neuter, or Intact

Here's a definition of cookie-cutter for you.

"Marked by lack of originality or distinction."

You're probably wondering where I'm going with this. Well, this is something that I want to be very clear on. You are certainly able to spay or neuter your German Shepherd whenever you want to. Is it a good idea to spay or neuter your pet early on in her life if you decide to? The answer is no. Do you have to spay or neuter your German Shepherd? The answer is no. So, with that out of the way let's delve into the pros and cons of whether to, and when.

For a long time, veterinarians recommended that all dogs be spayed or neutered at six months of age. It was a hard and fast rule. Why did they do this?

- Preventing unplanned litters
- Reduction of some health risks such as testicular cancer in males and life-threatening uterine infections in females
- Reducing behavioral problems like aggression and roaming

Now, however, many veterinarians and breeders have moved away from the early spay and neuter, cookie-cutter approach. They're recommending that German Shepherds, if you are going to spay or neuter at all, not be operated on until they are much older, somewhere in the sixteen-to-twenty-four-month age, or older. Why? There are several reasons, some particular to the GSD breed.

Delayed Spaying or Neutering

- German Shepherds don't reach their full physical maturity until they are two years old or later.

- Spaying or neutering before physical maturity significantly increases the risk of joint disorders like hip dysplasia and ligament tears.

- Increased likelihood of urinary incontinence in female German Shepherds spayed before one year old.

Early spaying or neutering removes the sexual hormones from the dog's body. Researchers believe that the sex hormones play a regulatory role in the growth process. Without the testosterone or estrogen, dogs will grow taller than normal with longer limbs. That's where the joint problems come into the picture.

Everyone will make their own decision based on individual circumstances. My German Shepherd is five years old, intact, and I have had no difficulties with him. He is not overly aggressive and does not "roam." We are responsible when out with him and he is closely monitored but he has never given us any cause for concern. So, I suggest you throw the cookie-cutter approach away. Consult with your vet and do what is best for your family.

Photo Courtesy of Andrea Liu

Hedging Your Bets

Before we barrel headlong into talking about pet insurance let's discuss money. If you acquire a GSD there is going to be some considerable financial outlay. So, don't go and pick up Schatzi expecting to buy food and the odd toy and that's it. There will be unexpected expenses, especially at the veterinarian. So German Shepherds and discretionary income go together. You just need to decide how to spend it.

Pet Insurance is a booming business. It works pretty much the way any insurance does.

- monthly premiums
- deductibles
- limitations on coverage

In calculating their premiums, the companies take a number of things into consideration.

- breed of dog
- your geographical location
- type of coverage
- age of dog

It's cheaper to get into the game early, so when you bring eight-week-old Schatzi home don't wait too long to make up your mind. If you dither and want to jump in later and your German Shepherd has a pre-existing condition your insurance company may not cover that. Your monthly premiums will go up as your GSD ages so you need to take that into account when working out whether pet insurance makes financial sense for you. Look at it this way. You can pay all at once without insurance or a little at a time with a policy.

Here's an alternative to insurance, because there is another way of financially buffering yourself from unexpected medical expenses with your GSD. You could set up a bank account and deposit a fixed amount each month. Consumer Reports says the average dog owner spends almost eight hundred dollars a year on vet costs for their pooch. That could be your guideline. You need to be faithful in the deposits though, or you're just setting yourself up for that big bill all at once with no cash reservoir.

We purchased pet insurance for Cody when he was a few months old. I have made claims several times. I grouse about the climbing premiums as he ages, but there is a term I've seen thrown around when talking about pets and medical expenses. It's something called "economic euthanasia." That's when owners have to put their German Shepherd down because they can't afford the medical bills. I never want to find myself in that position. What about you?

CHAPTER 19
Senior Citizen Challenges

I've always found dogs of all ages to be lots of fun. Exercise companions, nap buddies, conversational partners, mealtime fanatics, security team members, you name it, German Shepherds can continue to play many social roles as they age. Some of the best things about older dogs are they are calmer, they appreciate a domestic routine, they're still active but know how to take a break.

When I started out to write this chapter on older GSDs and what people might want to know about Shepherds in their senior years, I was hard put to define what a senior GSD is. Like people, ultimately the chronological age of a German Shepherd Dog is determined by how healthy they are, how physically fit they are. If we use the average life span range of a GSD, ten to thirteen years, then I conclude that Shepherds, on average, achieve senior status somewhere between seven and ten years old. Every dog is a unique individual and merits evaluation based on his physical and mental condition. Let's leave the numbers game alone now and move on to some of the things to pay attention to as Caesar ages.

Care Challenges

"There are lots of genetic issues in the breed so judicious health screening is important before the dogs are bred. Some of the genetic issues seen in the breed are: hip dysplasia, elbow dysplasia, congenital heart defects such as SAS, VSD, epilepsy, mesenteric torsion, GDV/bloat, exocrine pancreatic insufficiency, pannus, perianal fistulas, thyroid disease, degenerative myelopathy. Some of these diseases have health testing available and others require judicious screening and pedigree research by the breeder. Many of these genetic issues are incredibly expensive to manage or treat and some are even life threatening."

Katie Halfen
Casamoko Shepherds

First off, I want to mention some health care considerations that don't just pertain to senior German Shepherds, but to GSDs of any age. It's important to monitor your dog regularly because these afflictions can appear suddenly. If you catch things early, like a good partner, you can help maintain your dog's quality of life for many years.

Bloat

This is a serious condition that can kill your dog relatively quickly, but some simple routines can keep the chances of it happening to a minimum. In this disorder, air, digestive fluid, and gases are trapped in the stomach, causing the stomach to expand and often painfully twist. As the twisting takes place the blood flow is cut off. This is an emergency and immediate vet treatment is crucial. To help prevent bloat from happening, make the following list a daily habit. The risk of this happening unfortunately increases as the German Shepherd ages.

- Don't exercise Caesar for an hour before eating or an hour after a meal.

- Space your dog's food consumption out over the course of the day. Large meals can be a problem.

- GSDs love to drink water but curtail the marathon slurping sessions.

- Simethicone, a gas reducer, can be given to dogs to reduce bloating in an emergency. This is only a stopgap though, and you should still seek veterinarian help.

Exocrine Pancreatic Insufficiency (EPI)

EPI is a disorder that can show up in German Shepherds of any age. This disease disrupts the production of digestive enzymes by the pancreas or interferes with the use of those enzymes in the digestive system. Signs that your dog might have this problem are vomiting, diarrhea, increased appetite, and weight loss.

- Treatment for EPI is a digestive enzyme given to the dog at each meal for the rest of his life. Studies suggest EPI can be genetically inherited.

Degenerative Myelopathy

DM is a genetic disorder that usually affects mid-life or senior dogs. This neurologic disease results in progressive back end weakness that culminates in paralysis. There is no cure or effective treatment.

Osteoarthritis (OA)

This is commonly found in middle-aged and senior German Shepherds. OA frequently shows up in animals that have suffered from hip and elbow dysplasia. Bone spurs and thickening joint tissue cause pain and stiffness, restricting the dog's movement. The joint cartilage gradually deteriorates, and the condition is progressive. You might miss the early stages of this disease but if you think your dog is slowing down, just not being as active as he was, look for signs of OA.

HELPFUL TIP

Beds for Hip Dysplasia

Since German Shepherds are at a higher risk of developing hip dysplasia, it's useful to consider the type of bed you buy for your dog. Having a supportive bed can ease the pain associated with hip dysplasia. Look for beds that are labeled as orthopedic and suitable for large breed dogs. Thick memory foam mattresses provide extra support for your dog's joints. Choosing the right bed is just one small step in the treatment plan for hip dysplasia, so be sure to discuss your options with your vet.

- Limping and soreness
- Difficulty getting into the car
- Abnormal gait when walking
- Problems getting up after being resting

While there is no cure for OA there are some effective treatments that help keep your Shepherd's quality of life relatively high.

- Keeping your dog's weight down relieves pressure on the afflicted joints

- Physical therapy including heat and cold treatments
- Acupuncture
- Glucosamine and chondroitin sulfate may reduce inflammation

Perianal Fistula

Unfortunately found most often in German Shepherds, a perianal fistula is an abnormal, painful opening in the skin around the dog's anus. If untreated, these fistulae can expand into open wounds. Constipation, repeated licking of the anal area, and a foul odor are potential indicators of this problem.

- Surgery may be required to remove the fistulae
- Antibiotics could be required to treat infection
- Careful customization of diet can help control the disorder

von Willebrand Disease (vWD)

This is a bleeding disorder that involves a lack of clotting similar to hemophilia in humans. vWD is an inherited disorder. There are several symptoms that may indicate that your GSD has vWD.

- Excessive bleeding after injury or surgery
- Internal bleeding which shows as blood in the urine or feces
- Nosebleeds and bleeding from the gums

Blood transfusion is the main way of dealing with vWD. Some dogs can benefit from thyroid supplements if they are hypothyroid.

Pannus

Pannus is an immune-related condition affecting the dog's cornea or clear part of his eye. It first appears as redness and then what's known as the "third eyelid," or the corner of the eye, becomes swollen and in-flamed. It will typically affect both eyes. If left untreated Pannus will cause blindness.

- Steroidal eyedrops are recommended
- Avoid ultraviolet light

Treatment is not a cure but it usually stops progression of the disease.

Stayin' Alive

I know I've just bombarded you with a whack of information. It can be a little depressing if we don't give it some context. All those illnesses and disorders I've included in the first part of this chapter are out there and yes, they affect some German Shepherds. But the odds are that your dog, if he comes from a responsible breeder, will not be affected by any of the hereditary diseases. Some of the others can be managed quite well when caught early.

As your German Shepherd moves into his more mature years, there are a number of things you can do to help Caesar cope with the body changes aging brings. Let's start with diet.

Food First

Older dogs have slower metabolisms. It's a fact. That means the menu they've been working with up to this point in their lives may not be suitable for them anymore. When they start to have a less active lifestyle, after checking for any medical problems, you'll need to think about gradually changing the food, and the treats that are on offer in your house on a daily basis. Some veterinarians believe that heavier, overweight dogs age faster than leaner animals. That's something to consider about when food planning.

- High-quality protein. Caesar needs good protein now more than ever at this stage of life. German Shepherds are prone to muscle loss as they age so maintaining access to quality protein is a must.

- Easily digested food. Like a good quality control analyst, you need to monitor the input and output of your Shepherd's digestive system. People have eyed me strangely sometimes while I am examining my dog's poo but seriously you need to. Large, sloppy, stinky stools are signs that Caesar is not utilizing the nutrients in his food. Time to try something else.

- Carbohydrates. Dogs don't need a lot of carbs. Most commercial dog foods are overloaded with them. Excess carbs can contribute to weight gain, so closely monitoring the amount in your Shepherd's diet as he ages is a good thing. Treats don't escape the carb scrutiny here so pay attention as well to how many sweet potato chews you're handing out.

- Calories, period. I don't want to obsess about weight but if older dogs are moving less, and if that makes them prone to weight gain, then total calories need to be on your watch list. Commercial foods marketed to seniors can be calorie heavy or calorie light depending on the brand so you need to read the label.

- Dental issues? If your older German Shepherd has gum or teeth problems, you need to think about providing a softer food to eat. Hard kibble can sometimes exacerbate existing dental issues. Some commercial foods boast about their dental health benefits. Check with your vet for an opinion on them.

- Joint supplements and fatty acids. Humans take them and your older GSD can benefit from them as well. Adding glucosamine and chondroitin to a dog's diet can help with stiff joints related to arthritis. EPA and DHA fatty acids can help reduce inflammation.

Climate Control

When your dog is younger you don't necessarily spend much time thinking about whether the heat or cold is bothering him. Yes, he may need to hit the shade or go into the air conditioning and you don't want to leave Caesar outside too long on a winter day. But if you're like me you're not preoccupied with climate control and your German Shepherd. A senior dog is a whole other consideration.

- Older dogs, like older people, can lose the ability to maintain a constant body temperature because of changes in their metabolism. For instance, that means in hot weather, senior Shepherds might not be able to handle that long walk in the ninety-degree heat. Dehydration is also a concern. The same goes for the cold. You might have to put a sweater on that big, tough GSD.

Hitting the Bricks

Exercise is always important at any stage of life for your dog. You might have to scale it back as the years advance, especially if your senior German Shepherd has some health issues, but it's important to keep up those daily walks, for instance. You can still do many of the same things, just don't do them for as long. Look at it this way, your arm might be less sore on occasion from fewer ball tosses. You're OK with that, aren't you? A couple more words of advice.

- Break any exercise period into smaller chunks of time. That will give your older GSD time to recover between bouts of activity.

- Be less vigorous in your style of play. Slack off a little bit during the tug-of-war, for instance.

It's a State of Mind

As your dog ages and slows down, a natural inclination might be to leave him behind sometimes. "He's too slow" or "It will take too long" are familiar refrains from children sometimes. It's important to remember that older dogs need the stimulation of a trip to the store or a ride to the country just as much as younger German Shepherds. The picnics, family get-togethers, back yard parties are all opportunities to stimulate Caesar and keep him involved and motivated. While life keeps moving quickly and everyone seems busy, don't forget your dog. Including him makes for a healthy state of mind.

Grooming Your German & Vet Talk

Keeping a frequent, regular routine of grooming is even more important as your GSD ages. Older dogs and their senior immune systems get a boost if the regular brushing and combing carries on as well as washing his bedding frequently. Seniors might not be quite as fastidious about their personal hygiene as they once were so you can help them by staying on top of things. The hands-on approach during grooming also gives you a chance to run your hands over your dog's body and keep track of any changes that might be worthy of bringing to your vet's attention.

And speaking of the veterinarian, you should consider doubling down on that annual vet visit. Every six months is a better idea now because it will give you a jump on any problems that Caesar might be developing health wise. You can also discuss with your vet whether some of the suggested vaccinations actually need to be administered to an older dog. Rabies is usually state mandated, but you should have a frank chat with your vet about the others. An older dog's system may not tolerate the shots and boosters the way he did as a younger dog.

Aging Ailments

It's not an easy discussion to have but as your GSD ages you should be talking with family members about what I will call "eventualities." By that I mean some of the difficulties and diseases your senior dog can encounter as he enters the geriatric phase of his life. Let me go through some of the medical issues that you may have to deal with.

Obesity Alert

While obesity is something to be aware of during your dog's lifetime it's even more important to pay attention to in the later years. Any additional weight that your German Shepherd carries around increases the likelihood of high blood pressure, heart disease, and osteoarthritis. Some types of cancer are more prevalent in overweight and obese dogs.

Cancer

There are several cancers that are found more often in German Shepherds. Hemangiosacoma is one of them. This disease shows up most often as a tumor on the spleen or heart muscle. Surgery is sometimes possible but the prognosis is not generally good. Osteosarcoma is a bone cancer that is often found in large-breed dogs, including GSDs. It shows up generally on the long leg bones and amputation is the preferred treatment.

Cataracts

Cataracts, or a clouding of the eye lens, can develop at any age but older dogs are prone to the late onset variety. The condition does not necessarily develop at the same rate in both eyes. The clouding generally starts in the middle of the eye and spreads outward, eventually blinding the entire eye. Surgery is an expensive option but has a high success rate.

Dementia

You can call it dementia or canine cognitive dysfunction, but many owners may not notice the initial symptoms of mental impairment.

- Caesar may not sleep as well as he used to
- There could be lack of bladder or bowel control
- The dog may seem more anxious, more of the time
- Frequent pacing
- Barking and whining for no apparent reason

- Increased levels of aggression
- Loss of appetite
- Disorientation, even in familiar places

When you first start seeing any changes in your dog's behavior it's a good idea to keep notes. That will give you a timeline and specifics when you talk to your vet. Medication can be prescribed to help cope with some of the symptoms.

Canine Incontinence

There can be many different reasons for this disorder in older dogs. There are two sides to this condition.

1. Urinary incontinence. Signs can include excessive water consumption, dribbling urine, urinating large amounts, halting flow. In addition, spayed females may be more likely to experience urinary incontinence because of a lack of estrogen. Drugs are prescribed to help manage the condition. Surgery may also sometimes be required. Most German Shepherds respond well to treatment.

2. Fecal incontinence. Signs can include defecating in inappropriate places, bloated stomach, rear end tenderness, dragging rear on rug or floor. This condition is often caused by spinal cord disease and nerve damage. Treatment will depend on exact cause but prognosis can be optimistic.

Quality of Life

I will be completely upfront with you. This is the section of The Complete Guide to German Shepherds that I never wanted to write. Dealing with end-of-life decisions involving one of your most loved family members is extremely traumatic. There is the desire to hang on to what you have: you can't imagine the house without that big, old panting dog shambling around, toenails clicking on the hardwood floor. Wasn't he just a puppy last year? But the time always comes, sooner or later, when you have to ask yourself the hard questions. If German Shepherds could verbalize things, the process might be a whole lot easier. Even if they can't talk to you, they will certainly let you know how they're feeling. But you do have to pay attention to the signs and the most important thing in the whole equation is Caesar's quality of life. You can always be selfish and hang onto something, but maybe, just maybe, it's time to let go.

Tough Questions

If you find yourself asking some tough questions, then you know something out of the ordinary is going on in your German Shepherd's life. Maybe he's not participating as enthusiastically in some of the routines he's enjoyed all his life. I can't imagine my dog, Cody, not wanting to run after the ball or attempt with all his might to win a tug-of-war battle. But that's when the tough questions will begin. You might be facing a terminal illness with your dog, or the aftermath of an accident, or he could be nearing the end of his life—the same factors come into play in your decision making on whether it's time to say good-bye.

Pain Threshold

One of the major indicators in deciding whether it's time to let your dog go is how much pain Caesar is in. Dogs don't always let you know how bad they're feeling. That's because they can't imagine anything other than right now, and if they see a friendly face walk into the room, they're likely to wag their tail even if they are in a lot of discomfort. So, the pain threshold determination is up to you. Here are some things to watch for.

- Disproportionate amount of crying or groaning
- Uncontrolled trembling
- No interest in drinking or eating
- Heavy panting
- Restlessness

Gut Factor

This is where you need to separate you and your dog. What is good for you, what is good for Caesar. Get as close to dispassionate as possible (it's not really possible but imagine you can) and look at all the signs that are staring you in the face. Is your dog eating, what kind of appetite is he exhibiting? Even picky eaters, like some GSDs are, have to eat, enjoy eating, some of the time. If there is no enjoyment at mealtime, the treats aren't vacuumed up as usual, that's telling you something. Behavioral changes are another indicator. If the animal doesn't seem to enjoy very much, there is a lack of zest for things in general, that's another sign. And the thing that puts them all together is your gut, your intuition. I'm an advocate of talking to your dog. Sit down and have a conversation with him. Sometimes that helps you work things out in your own mind. Listen to what you're saying. Listen to what they're saying.

The Decision

If you're listening to yourself, honestly, and you realize your GSD is in a lot of pain, then you have part of your answer about letting go. That's what your dog is feeling. The flip side of that is how are you feeling? Knowing that it is the right thing to do sometimes isn't enough. You have to be able to bring yourself to detach, to be able to say to yourself that letting go is the right thing to do. To complicate things, you may have all kinds of people weighing in with their opinions, including family members, and they have a right to be part of the discussion. But they can't make you feel guilty. Hopefully you can come to a collective decision but if you can't you still need to go with what your gut is telling you is the right thing to do.

Lastly, you will have to roll into the mix what your vet is telling you. If she is advocating some kind of treatment then you have to give strong consideration to that. If she's advising that it's time to euthanize Caesar, then you need to consider that. There is always going to be a whole lot of guilt and sadness, that's normal. The bottom line is doing what your gut is telling you is the right thing to do. No one can help you with that decision.

How to Deal with Grief

When the decision to euthanize your German Shepherd is being made, you may feel a creeping sense of loss, grief setting in, before Caesar is even gone. I'm not a believer in the so-called five stages of grief that Elisabeth Kubler-Ross made famous. She theorized that we all pass through different "phases" during and after the death of a loved one.

1. Denial
2. Anger
3. Bargaining
4. Depression
5. Acceptance

I think that most of us follow our own timeline. You may experience some of the five stages in order or out of order, but certainly number four, depression, will be experienced by most of us. I'm not sure if I could ever get to "acceptance."

My dog makes me a more social being. Cody is my confidant. He doesn't share any of my secrets so he has my complete trust. He also has the solution to many of life's problems. Most of the time that entails taking a long walk and not thinking about anything other than the passing scenery. So how do we deal with our grief when that big German Shepherd face is no longer there to help us navigate through life?

Let It Happen

The first days of life after GSD will be incredibly hard and you just have to let them happen. Grieving is an individual process. Those feelings you have that make you want to withdraw and stare out the window are perfectly natural. But as you're doing that you need to, slowly, maybe just a little bit at a time, think about what's next. What is going to happen in your life now?

- Even if you think you might get another dog in the near future, rearrange things around the house so you don't have to see the reminders of a missing presence. The food and water bowl should be put away for now, and the bed in the porch should be picked up. You're not dishonoring Caesar's memory. You're not wiping out his existence, you're just moving on.

- Write yourself a letter about your dog. Or just write a free-flowing story of whatever you want to include about your late pet's life. Chances are it will be a compilation of all the good things, even those late nights with the puppy crying when he first came home. That's all good stuff and it may make you cry but that's all right. Think about the positives.

- Recognize that grief is just an extension of love for your dog. He gave you his love unconditionally and he would be happy to see that you loved him enough to grieve for him. I could be accused of anthropomorphizing here but it's just what I think.

- Your GSD gave you a sense of purpose while he was alive and there is a legacy purpose there too. He made you a stronger person by helping you cope with life. That's a present he gave to you and you need to move forward with that gift.

One of the best things about German Shepherds is they are always in the present. That way they never miss anything going on around them. They don't walk around with their head in the clouds thinking about next week. They don't even know there is a next week. So, if you live in the present, with Caesar's memory in your heart, you can never lose him. You know he would love you even more for being able to do that.

Remember what I told you at the beginning of this book? That when you bring a German Shepherd puppy home you are in for the ride of your life? And that they will love you and never leave you? It's all true.

My Tip
➢ Love your dog. Give them a hug for me.

Made in United States
Troutdale, OR
01/13/2025

27872921R20106